Ru

Contents

▌*Opposite: Pushkin in a pensive mood.*

This Way Russia

A New Lease of Life

There could hardly be a more exciting time to visit Russia, a nation emerging from the throes of a vast political and cultural upheaval. The whole approach to tourism has changed. Places previously off limits are now on view; cities have regained their pre-Soviet names; streets have been relabelled. In all this turmoil, the glories of Russia have been revealed as if from behind a screen, more accessible than ever before. Many have been brilliantly restored, although funds are scarce and much remains to be done. Moscow and St Petersburg can now offer hotels with Western standards of service and comfort—at a price—as well as a wide range of more modest accommodation. Restaurants too have multiplied in number and variety, from Japanese to Georgian, and some of them are within reach of ordinary Russians, which makes them a bargain for the visitor.

In the cataclysm of the early 1990s, freedom of speech, religion, movement and trade came with bewildering suddenness. Young people, especially in the big cities, abandoned the communist past with scarcely a backward glance, not only to indulge a taste for sharp fashion and anarchic rock groups, but to seize new business opportunities as well. Privately owned enterprises sprang up; private housing developments mushroomed in the most desirable suburbs of the cities, though the source of much of this new wealth is of doubtful legality, to say the least. The liberated media—including commercial TV channels—compete with the best and worst of the West in frankness and sensationalism.

Westernization is not the only trend. Traditions are also being revived. Churches and cathedrals, used for 70 years as museums or warehouses, or just allowed to crumble into ruins, are being restored and re-opened all over the country. Robed priests never appeared in public during the Soviet era; now they are part of the street scene. Some young people are choosing the monastic life, formerly forbidden, and reclaiming some of the monasteries and convents.

Land of Extremes

Throughout history, Russia has oscillated between openness and secrecy in its relations with the outside world and its attitudes

Graffiti is rare in Russia, but a wall in Arbat Street has been appropriated as a memorial to Viktor Tsoy, a rock star who died in 1990.

have ranged from welcoming Western ideas and technology to self-reliance or hostility. Another pattern has been set, and still holds good today: Russian rulers have either been forceful—often to excess—or weak to the point of feebleness. Conditions have swung between the extremes of order and disorder, individual behaviour between decorum and *skandal*, the national mood from elation to despair and back again, all with extraordinary speed.

The collapse of the Soviet Union was just such a violent change. Its people found their world turned upside-down. The empire put together in tsarist times was no more, and millions of Russians had to come back to a "home" they had never known. Savings, wages and pensions were wiped out in a ten-thousand-fold decline in the value of the rouble. Old people who had felt secure found themselves reduced to penury, forced to sell whatever little they owned in order to survive. Although more goods did appear in the shops, few could afford them. In the privatization of state-owned industries (and that meant practically everything), the well-placed and unscrupulous grabbed as much as they could. Employees were allocated shares, but many sold them for a pittance at a time when they were desperate to raise some money. Others found they owned nothing but a worthless scrap of paper when "their" factory or business was closed down. It's no wonder that many hanker after the comparative security of the Soviet past: every election has shown the strength of support for communist candidates, or nationalists who dream of rebuilding the USSR.

Enduring the Intolerable

A sort of stability has been restored, but beneath the long-suffering surface, don't be surprised to find widespread resentment at what has happened. Highly qualified, hard-working people are making the equivalent of 30 US dollars a week. How do they survive? Some have a vegetable plot where they can grow food, others moonlight. Many still benefit from the remnants of the socialist system in the form of low-cost housing and public services. Inevitably, prostitution is a highly visible feature of the big cities. Perhaps only the legendary Russian capacity to endure the intolerable prevents an explosion, or maybe the pragmatic realisation that another revolution would only make matters worse.

As in the old days of the American Wild West, the strong, the clever and the well-protected rule the roost and divide the spoils. And yet there is light amid the gloom. The enigmatic new president, Vladimir Putin, has promised a crackdown on corruption, and popular support for his policies leads to the hope of more stable government in the future. His election in March 2000 at last brought down the curtain on the Yeltsin era.

Foreign companies which have invested in Russia and held on tightly through all the difficulties praise the high levels of education and irrepressible enthusiasm of their young Russian employees. It is in the new generation that hope lies.

1

THE GREATEST MUSEUM In the scale, scope and magnificence of its collections, especially of Western Art, St Petersburg's **Hermitage** has no equal. With several hundred galleries and millions of exhibits, the Hermitage is vast, rich and daunting. But don't miss it. For your first visit, the best thing is to take a guided tour, available in several languages.

5

Flashback

Small Beginnings

The harsh grip of its winters deterred settlement of northern Russia for a thousand years, while empires flourished to the south and west. Vikings from Scandinavia ranged along its rivers, sometimes in search of plunder but more often of trade—in furs, amber and precious metals. Among them, the Viking Chief Rurik made Novgorod his base in AD 862. His successor Oleg moved south to Kiev, which grew to be the capital of a large state, the Kievan Rus.

In 988, Vladimir I, a convert to Christianity, invited monks from Constantinople to establish a mission, a step that led to the creation of the Russian Orthodox Church. They also introduced Cyrillic script, a version of the Greek alphabet and forerunner of today's Russian alphabet. In the 11th century, under the rule of Yaroslav the Wise, the prestige of the Kievan Rus was at its zenith.

Under attack from the east, Kievan Rus declined in the late 11th century, but its northern

The cathedral of St Peter and St Paul at Peterhof was used as a cinema during the Soviet era.

outposts—Suzdal, Vladimir and Rostov the Great—flourished. Moscow was a latecomer. It was founded in 1147 by Yuri Dolgoruky ("Longarm"), son of Vladimir II of Kiev. The court moved to Vladimir in 1169, followed by the patriarchs of the Russian church.

Tatar Rule

Early in the 13th century, the armies of Genghis Khan swept down from Mongolia and overran Central Asia. They were soon at the gates of Europe. Russian resistance was quickly crushed; only Novgorod in the northern marshes held out. Its prince, Alexander, made peace with the Tatars (as the Russians called the Mongols) to face another threat, that of the Swedish and German Teutonic Knights, nominally "crusaders" but more concerned with land and loot than religion. Alexander's small army defeated them by the Neva river, gaining him the name Nevsky, and eventually sainthood.

The vast empire of the Mongols soon broke up. The Russian towns came under the Golden Horde, based on the Volga river. Instead of occupying them, the Tatars used local rulers (Alexander Nevsky was set up as Grand Prince of Vladimir) to gather taxes, and only intervened to crush signs of rebellion.

Moscow Takes Over

In 1325, Ivan Kalita ("Money-bags") moved the capital to Moscow. Prince Dmitry defeated the Tatars near the Don river in 1380, earning the title Donskoy, although it was another 100 years before the Russians under Ivan III (the Great) finally threw off the Tatar yoke. Ivan quadrupled the area under his rule but failed in one objective—to gain an outlet on the Baltic Sea. Indeed, in taking Novgorod and expelling its traders (mainly German and Scandinavian), he closed the main link with the West. Russia became inward-looking and isolated for the next two centuries.

The fall of Constantinople to the Turks in 1453 led Russians to think of Moscow as the true centre of the Orthodox Church. Ivan saw himself as successor to the Byzantine line, adopting the double-headed imperial eagle symbol and marrying the niece of the last emperor. He began to be known as tsar, a word derived from Caesar.

Ivan the Terrible

Vasily III followed his father Ivan the Great in adding to the national territory, but he died in 1533, when his son Ivan IV was only three years old. The boy's

FROM RURIK TO PUTIN			
Rurik	862–79	Catherine II	1762–96
Oleg	882–912	(the Great)	
Vladimir I	980–1015	Alexander I	1801–25
Yaroslav (the Wise)	1019–54	Nicholas I	1825–55
Yuri Dolgoruky	1149–57	Alexander II	1855–81
Alexander Nevsky	1252–63	Alexander III	1881–94
Ivan I (Kalita)	1325–40	Nicholas II	1894–1917
Dmitry Donskoy	1359–89	Lenin	1917–24
Ivan III (the Great)	1462–1505	Stalin	1927–53
Vasily III	1505–33	Khrushchev	1957–64
Ivan IV (the Terrible)	1547–84	Brezhnev	1964–82
Boris Godunov	1598–1605	Andropov	1982–84
Mikhail Romanov	1613–45	Chernenko	1984–85
Peter I (the Great)	1689–1725	Gorbachev	1985–91
Anna	1730–40	Yeltsin	1991–99
Elizabeth	1741–62	Putin	2000

mother Yelena acted as regent, but power was in the hands of feuding nobles, or boyars, whom Ivan came to hate. At 16, he was crowned tsar in the Kremlin's Uspensky Cathedral, where the coronations of all his successors were held until the monarchy was overthrown in 1917.

Tempered by a happy marriage, he ruled at first with comparative restraint. Only after his first wife Anastasia died in 1560 did he embark on the reign of terror remembered in his name (in Russian, *Grozny*, or Awesome). His opponents, real or imagined, became the victims of mass executions; the head of the Russian Church was strangled on his orders; cities sacked and burned and their people killed on the slightest suspicion of disloyalty.

Much of Ivan's dirty work was carried out by the *Oprichniki,* his private army of cut-throats. Dressed in black and wearing the emblem of a dog's head, they seized land and whole towns, torturing and murdering priests and boyars. In 1581, Ivan killed his eldest son in a fit of rage. Also called Ivan, he was apparently as vicious as his father, but afterwards the tsar was filled with remorse. In his last years his blood lust abated; he even stood down as tsar for two years and lived privately, brooding on his sins. He died in 1584, leaving his kingdom to his elder surviving son Fyodor; his infant son Dmitry was sent to Uglich on the Volga.

Time of Troubles

Bad as conditions may have been under Ivan the Terrible, worse was to come. Fyodor, 27 when he succeeded, was described by the English envoy Giles Fletcher as "simple and slowe-witted, but verie gentle, merciful, of no martiall disposition." A blessed relief, perhaps, to the Russian people, but not the man to rule them. The power behind the throne was Boris Godunov, a favourite of Ivan the Terrible and a calculating politician.

Fyodor had no children and when his nine-year-old brother Dmitry was found with his throat cut in 1591, Godunov was suspected of ordering the murder. The people of Uglich lynched his agents, and Godunov retaliated with mass executions, conveniently silencing any witnesses. When Fyodor died in 1598, Boris Godunov was proclaimed tsar. His rivals, the Romanovs, were banished to distant monasteries.

Years of crop failures led to famine and anarchy. Then in 1604 a young man claiming to be none other than Dmitry gathered support in Poland and marched on Moscow, while Boris sat in the Kremlin, steeped in gloom. He suddenly died in 1605, just in time to avoid humiliation. The army went over to False Dmitry, who rode into Moscow on a white horse as crowds cheered and church bells tolled. Ivan the Terrible's widow recognized him as her son and he was crowned tsar, but within a year he was assassinated and replaced by Vasily Shuysky, the new favourite of the Moscow rabble.

More false Dmitrys appeared on the scene. One set up a rival court near Moscow with the first pretender's wife as his own tsarina. In 1610, Shuysky was captured by the Poles, who occupied Moscow, while the king of Poland claimed the throne. Russian boyars, church leaders and people were at last stirred into united action. The Poles were thrown out, and a national assembly met in 1613 to select a new tsar, the 16-year-old Mikhail Romanov. First he had to be found—at a monastery in Kostroma on the Volga—and then persuaded to take on a task which had proved fatal to its recent holders. Finally he agreed, founding a dynasty which was to rule until the end of the monarchy in 1917.

Looking Westwards

When the third of the Romanovs, Fyodor III, died childless in 1682, his brother Ivan should have succeeded. But Ivan was only 16 and feeble-minded; he and his half-brother Peter, aged nine, were declared joint tsars, with their elder sister Sophia as regent.

Peter was a lively and confident child. He built his own boat and learned to sail; he drilled his family's servants and turned them into a useful private army. At 17, he was ready to challenge his ambitious sister. Fearing her supporters in Moscow, he set up his court at the Trinity Monastery of St Sergius. Ministers, church leaders and army officers joined him and soon the issue was decided. Sophia was locked up in Novodevichy Convent and Peter reigned alone. Ivan was treated kindly until his death in 1696.

Influenced by his friends and drinking companions among the foreign community, Peter was determined to modernize his country. He set off on an 18-month visit to western Europe in 1697, the first ever by a tsar. Despite his 250-strong entourage, he insisted on travelling incognito as Peter Mikhailov, though his height of 2 m (6 ft 7 in) made him difficult to miss. He worked with ship's carpenters in Holland, observed dissections, sailed to England with the Royal Navy, studied navigation and science, argued with bishops and wrecked his London lodgings.

Back in Russia, as a symbol of Western ways Peter personally cut off the beards of his ministers and banned traditional robes from the court. He set up a civil service, started the first newspapers, opened schools, and established mines and factories. His great ambition was to build a port on the Baltic, as Russia's "window on the West", and create a Russian navy. Sweden blocked the way, but in the Northern War (1700–21) which he launched to seize the land he needed, Peter's forces captured a foothold at the mouth of the Neva.

The construction of St Petersburg began in 1703, and building was far enough advanced for the tsar to transfer the capital from Moscow in 1712. Only an autocrat of Peter's demonic energy could have achieved such results. Unnumbered serfs, prisoners of war and convicts struggled to drain the marshes using simple tools or their bare hands, and tens of thousands died. The tsar dragooned princes as well as paupers, forcing them to move to his new capital and build palaces at their own expense.

After final victory over Sweden, Peter's tame senate pressed on him the titles of Emperor and "Peter the Great". He died in 1725, having turned a backward nation into one of the most powerful on earth.

Era of Empresses

Peter the Great had not named a successor. Sickly, feeble and lazy, his son Alexis had been everything his father detested. Peter threatened to disinherit him, then to force him to become a monk. Alexis fled to Vienna but was enticed back by false promises, tortured and beaten to death. Peter was therefore briefly succeeded by his widow Catherine, although real power was in the hands of Prince Menshikov.

Peter's niece Anna reigned from 1730–40, but relied on German ministers to do the work. The pattern continued with his daughter Elizabeth, a voluptuous beauty with her father's energy, though she employed it more in love affairs than affairs of state.

TWO SUPERB SUMMER PALACES The retreats built outside St Petersburg for the tsars and empresses by French, Italian and British architects grew to be just as opulent as their palaces in the city. Peter the Great's **Peterhof** and the Catherine Palace at **Tsarskoe Selo** (Pushkin) are two of the most spectacular.

11

The foolish, childish Peter III who came to the throne in 1761 was deposed six months later in favour of his wife, a German-born princess who became Empress Catherine II, "the Great". (Peter's murder soon afterwards was probably not ordered by her, though it was certainly convenient.) Like Elizabeth, Catherine took a string of lovers, but unlike her, was determined to rule as well as reign. The empire expanded to the west and south, and she travelled to see the new lands. She corresponded with kings and philosophers, promoted the arts and founded the Hermitage Museum in St Petersburg.

Catherine's successor Paul, said to be her son by an early lover Saltykov, ruled by whim, ordering floggings and banishment to Siberia for the slightest offence. In 1801 he was strangled in a palace coup, possibly with the foreknowledge of his son, who became Emperor Alexander I.

Napoleon's Big Mistake

In the Napoleonic Wars, Russia joined the coalition against France, but was forced to make peace in 1807 after the French emperor had beaten her allies the Prussians. Two years later Russia gained Finland from the Swedes, but France set up a puppet state in Poland which soon caused friction. Napoleon resolved to knock out his only rival on the European mainland, and in June 1812, the largest army ever assembled marched on Moscow. The Russians avoided battle until August 26, when the two sides clashed at Borodino, 130 km (80 miles) west of Moscow. Both suffered huge losses, but it was the Russians who withdrew and the French claimed victory.

Napoleon rode into Moscow, but not in triumph. The city had been abandoned by the population and was burning. Two-thirds of the houses were destroyed; there was little food. Napoleon waited six weeks for emissaries from Tsar Alexander to negotiate terms, but none came. Finally, as winter approached, he ordered the retreat. Harried by the better-equipped Russians and hampered by snow, frozen and starving, fewer than one in ten survived.

Missed Chances

The Russian army pursued Napoleon all the way to Paris, and Alexander took a major role at the peace conferences. Many of the younger officers picked up liberal ideas in the west, and when Alexander died they called for a constitutional monarchy and freedom for the serfs. In December 1825, they paraded in St Petersburg, but lacking leadership or a plan of action, the Decembrists, as they became known, were shot down or disarmed by troops loyal to the new tsar, Nicholas I. His 30-year reign was a period of severe repression, intended to prevent the revolutionary virus which had spread through Europe from infecting Russia. Political police spied on dissidents; censors hounded reformist writers.

At first Alexander II took a softer line than his father, and in 1861 he signed a decree emancipating the serfs, the landowners' peasant slaves. It was his intention that they should be given some land, but millions received nothing. Worse off than before, many drifted to the cities. Underground opposition parties began to organize, and the tsar ordered his ministers to crack down. He was assassinated by bomb-throwing anarchists in 1881 as he drove through St Petersburg. His son and successor Alexander III responded with more repression. Revolutionaries were executed or imprisoned; many liberals were exiled.

Road to Revolution

The reign of Nicholas II began with an ill omen, when crowds at his coronation in 1896 stampeded and 1,200 were crushed to death.

At the turn of the century Russia seemed docile, but

Red Square in the heart of Moscow.

The 16th-century Novodevichy Convent, reflected in the Moskva river, is hauntingly beautiful.

beneath the surface opposition was gathering strength. A disastrous war with Japan exposed government incompetence and discredited the autocracy. In January 1905, more than 200,000 people gathered in St Petersburg to petition the tsar for a democratic assembly, but soldiers fired on the crowd, killing at least 100 in an incident known as Bloody Sunday. Strikes and riots broke out all over the country. The tsar agreed to the election of a State Duma, or parliament, although it was far from democratic and he could veto its decisions.

War with Germany in 1914 brought heavy defeats. Empress Alexandra, German-born, was a focus of unpopularity, which her association with the dissolute peasant Rasputin did nothing to dispel. Her son Alexei was a haemophiliac and the "holy man" seemed able to stop his bleeding, but she also urged Nicholas to take Rasputin's advice on political and military appointments.

In February 1917, riots broke out in St Petersburg (known by then as Petrograd, to sound more Russian). The Duma defied the tsar and set up a provisional government. Nicholas took the decision to abdicate; he and his family were placed under house arrest and later shot. Revolutionary leaders including Lenin and Trotsky returned from abroad, and their Bolshevik party took control of the "soviets", or workers' committees. The Bolsheviks seized the Winter Palace in October, 1917, and arrested the provisional government. Soviets in other cities followed suit, though there was a week of fighting before they controlled Moscow.

The Soviet Union

Renamed the Communist Party, the Bolsheviks moved the capital back to Moscow in 1918. They signed a humiliating peace with Germany, leaving the new Red Army under Trotsky free to fight the White forces who opposed the Bolshevik revolution. Many parts of the former Russian Empire had broken away, and it took three years of bitter civil war to recapture them.

In 1924, Lenin died, without saying who should succeed him, apart from expressing his distrust of Joseph Stalin, the General Secretary of the Communist Party. Nevertheless, Stalin managed to isolate and discredit his rivals and emerge as undisputed leader. Like Ivan the Terrible centuries before, he saw—or claimed to see—treachery everywhere. The Revolution began to consume its own, with show trials of its leaders who "confessed" to ridiculous charges and were duly executed.

In wave after wave of purges, millions of ordinary citizens were sent to labour camps in the Arctic and Siberia. Few ever returned.

Stalin signed a pact with Nazi Germany in 1939, but Hitler was only biding his time. On June 22, 1941, he launched a huge attack on the Soviet Union, hoping, like Napoleon before him, for a quick victory. But this was only the start of a titanic four-year struggle, costing perhaps 40 million lives. At first, things seemed to go well for the Germans. By October they were close to Moscow and had besieged Leningrad (St Petersburg), but an early winter slowed them to a standstill before they could take either. In the Russians they found an enemy as ruthless as themselves, and able to call on vast reserves. At Stalingrad (Volgograd), the turning point of the war, a whole German army was encircled and destroyed.

The Red Army occupied eastern Europe and installed communist regimes there. The Cold War began, and with it an expensive arms race with the West. When Stalin died in 1953, life in the Soviet Union took a turn for the better; the new party leader Nikita Khrushchev denounced Stalin's crimes in 1956. The first *Sputnik* satellite the following year and Yuri Gagarin's orbital flight in 1961 impressed the

15

world, but after disastrous harvests and foreign policy setbacks Khrushchev was forced to resign in 1964.

Stagnation and Collapse

As party boss and then president, Leonid Brezhnev aimed to preserve the status quo. In 1968 the Soviet army crushed the "Prague Spring" pro-democracy movement in Czechoslovakia, and in 1979 they invaded Afghanistan to prop up a communist government. At home the ageing Brezhnev presided over a moribund economy in which up to 40 per cent of the national wealth was spent on the armed forces, with much of the rest wasted through inefficiency and corruption.

When Brezhnev at last died, in 1982, he was followed by Yuri Andropov, the former KGB chief. But he was already a sick man, and died only 14 months later. Next in the pecking order was the decrepit Konstantin Chernenko, who lasted a mere year before joining the line of graves beside the Kremlin wall.

The energy and comparative youth of his successor, Mikhail Gorbachev, were a refreshing change, as he moved among crowds in the street and debated with them face to face. His catchwords were *glasnost* (openness) and *perestroika* (restructuring), but he believed that they could be achieved through reform of the existing system. Inevitably, the Communist Party split, with the old guard in one camp, liberals in another, leaving Gorbachev with no power base.

In 1991, in the first direct election of its kind, Boris Yeltsin was voted president of the Russian Federation, by far the biggest of the USSR's 15 republics. As the old order crumbled, the others seized the chance to assert their independence. Hardliners sent tanks on to the Moscow streets, but vast crowds turned out to protest.

Outside the "White House", seat of the Russian parliament, Yeltsin climbed on a tank and denounced the coup attempt. Its leaders were arrested, the Communist Party was banned in Russia and its property seized. Gorbachev had been marginalized, but his proposal to replace the Soviet Union by a loose alliance, the Commonwealth of Independent States (CIS), was agreed. On December 21, 1991, the red flag was hauled down and the USSR ceased to exist. Gorbachev resigned four days later.

Russia Reborn

Boris Yeltsin and his ministers wanted to move quickly to a free-market economy, but the parliament blocked their proposals. In 1993, Yeltsin declared it dissolved, but the communists (now legalized again) and nationalists who dominated it defied him. Moscow watched in amazement as tanks shelled the White House and troops stormed it.

A new assembly called the State Duma was then elected. A majority still opposed the president, but a new constitution gave him greater powers to overrule it and reform continued. Russia still faces daunting problems. The government is bankrupt. Taxes go uncollected; wages in the remaining state industries, civil service and armed forces are often months late. Corruption and organized crime is said to be involved in 70 per cent of all business activity. Russia's vast natural resources—oil, gas and minerals—are practically its only source of income, but much of the revenue is illegally diverted abroad. Huge international loans stabilized the rouble for a while, inflation was brought under control and privatization gave entrepreneurs a chance to shine. In 1998, this modest progress was thrown into reverse when it became clear that Russia could not repay even the interest on its debts to Western banks. The rouble plummeted and a procession of ministers appointed and sacked by Boris Yeltsin backed away from free market policies but failed to find any alternative remedies.

On December 31, 1999, Yeltsin stepped down from the presidency. His prime minister Vladimir Putin, a former KGB officer and head of the domestic intelligence service, took over. Promising to crush the separatist rebellion in Chechnya and to restore Russia to a place of respect among the world's great nations, he immediately won the support of the people, who re-elected him in March 2004. The Orthodox Church has asserted itself as a political as well as spiritual force: in 2000, the last tsar of Russia, Nicholas II, was made a saint.

17

On the Scene

Most visits to Russia begin either in Moscow or St Petersburg, two contrasting cities whose size, facilities, historic resonance and extraordinary art collections set them apart from the rest. Excursions to the countryside reveal a different and much older face: villages of tiny wooden houses, ancient churches and walled monasteries, set in a flat landscape of forests, meadows and wide, slow rivers. This guide also covers the sights of the Golden Ring, east of Moscow, and river cruises.

▶ MOSCOW

The Kremlin, Around Red Square, Central Moscow – West and South, Outskirts – North and East

When Prince Yuri Dolgoruky fenced in a low hill just north of the Moskva river in the 12th century, his settlement was one of many in the region. It eventually eclipsed its rivals through diplomacy, avoiding conflict with the Tatar overlords until it was strong enough to defy them. After Ivan III (the Great) built the Russian State into a substantial power, Moscow expanded rapidly.

It remained the guardian of tradition, symbol of Russia's Ortho-dox, Slav and Asian connections even after Peter the Great had made St Petersburg his capital and pointed the nation's face to the West. In 1918, the new Bolshevik rulers moved back to Moscow, seeing it as safer from foreign intervention.

A street plan of Moscow looks something like a spider's web, with the Kremlin at the heart of several concentric thoroughfares. Next out from the centre, the line of a 16th-century rampart is followed today by the Boulevard Ring, an arc of twin avenues with gardens along the middle. Beyond this, a 15-km (9-mile) circle of outer defences became the

Like colourful oriental turbans, the domes of St Basil's Cathedral cover nine chapels.

Garden Ring, a busy traffic artery. The most recent addition to the map is the 110-km (68-mile) Outer Ring Road, marking the city limit.

The Kremlin

The word kremlin *(kreml)* means a fortress or walled town; the one in Moscow is the biggest and most famous of all. The earliest rampart was of earth and wood, but successive rulers raised and strengthened the defences after every attack; the present brick walls date from the 1490s, though they have been frequently restored.

When the court and government moved to St Petersburg in 1712, the Kremlin was demoted to ceremonial status. Twenty-five years later, its last wooden buildings burned down. In the next major disas-

ter, the French occupation and fire of 1812, much of the Kremlin was luckily saved or at least restorable.

Each of the 20 towers along the wall has its own history and architectural quirks. Best known is the 67-m (220-ft) Spassky (Saviour) Tower, facing Red Square between St Basil's Cathedral and Lenin's Tomb. Its bells, weighing up to 2 tonnes, are heard regularly on Moscow Radio chiming the quarter hours. Before the 1917 revolution, those passing through Spassky Gate had to doff their hats.

The visitor entrance today is by way of the Kutafya Tower, standing clear of the western wall, and then through the Trinity (*Troitskaya*) Gate, beneath the tallest tower. (The usual exit is the Borovitsky Gate in the southwest corner.) The soldiers who stand guard at the war memorial outside the western wall live in the Arsenal, inside on the left.

Bell Tower of Ivan the Great

Ahead, the white belfry with a golden onion dome *(Kolokolnya Ivana Velikogo),* was begun in the early 1500s and raised to its present height of 80 m (263 ft) a century later to serve as a lookout post. It's the tallest structure in the Kremlin. The largest of the 21 bells is in the adjoining shorter tower and weighs 64 tonnes. The 200-tonne

Tsar Bell at the foot of the tower is the world's biggest, cast in 1733–35 by the father-and-son team, Ivan and Mikhail Motorin. Sadly, it was cracked in a fire before it could be hung; the piece that fell out still lies next to it.

To the north of the bell tower stands the colossal Tsar Cannon cast in 1586, during the reign of Fyodor I, whose image is on the barrel. It was intended to fire stone shot, not the iron balls now beside it, but it seems that nobody ever had the courage to use the monster.

Archangel Cathedral

Between the bell tower and the Kremlin's south wall, the small, five-domed *Arkhangelsky Sobor,* dedicated to the Archangel Michael, was completed in 1508. It combined Italian and Russian artistic traditions, opening new prospects for Russian architecture, and was used for the weddings and burials of the tsars. The church contains 46 royal tombs including those of Ivan the Great and the first of the Romanov dynasty, Mikhail. Ivan the Terrible's tomb is hidden away, but one of the attendants may open a door to reveal it.

Cathedral of the Annunciation

On the opposite side of Cathedral Square, *Blagoveshchensky Sobor* was built in fits and starts in the 15th and 16th centuries. This was the private church of the tsars; the interior is rather subdued and intimate. Its priceless icons include works by Theophanes the Greek, painted in the late 14th century, and his illustrious pupil Rublyov.

Cathedral of the Assumption

Every tsar from the 15th century onwards was crowned in *Uspensky Sobor*, the burial place of most heads of the Russian Church from the 14th to the 18th centuries. The present building with its golden helmet domes and semicircular gables was designed by the Italian architect Fioravanti and built in the 1470s. The interior is vivid, in gold, silver, red, purple and blue, and packed with works of art and historical relics; the icons include treasures from as early as the 12th century.

The Kremlin Palaces

A cluster of small gilded domes tops the 17th-century Terem Palace *(Teremnoy Dvorets)*, next to the little single-domed Church of the Deposition of the Robe *(Tserkov Rizpolozheniya)*, near the west door of the Assumption Cathedral. The middle window in the Throne Room is the "petition window" from which a box was lowered to anyone wishing to put a request to the tsar.

THREE CELEBRATED CEMETERIES Composers, writers and disgraced Soviet leaders are buried at **Novodevichy Convent** in Moscow; famous figures from the Soviet era lie next to the **Kremlin Wall** near Lenin's Tomb, the tombs of many 19th-century composers and writers can be seen at **Alexander Nevsky Monastery** in St Petersburg.

Facing Cathedral Square, the Palace of Facets *(Granovitaya Palata)* is a ceremonial hall built in 1491 by the Italian architects Ruffo and Solari; the name comes from the geometric carving of the renaissance stonework of its exterior.

Unless you happen to be invited to a state reception, you have little chance of seeing the lavish interior of the 19th-century Grand Kremlin Palace *(Bolshoy Kremlyovsky Dvorets)* adjoining the Annunciation Cathedral and Palace of Facets. It appears to have three storeys. In fact there are only two; the two top rows of windows serve the same rooms.

In incongruous contrast to the rest of the Kremlin buildings, the State Kremlin Palace *(Gosudarstvenny Kremlyovsky Dvorets)* is a white marble-and-glass block built in 1961 to hold Communist Party congresses. It can seat 6,000 people and has been used for concerts and ballet performances—there's a good view from every seat in the house.

Patriarch's Palace

Next to the Tsar Cannon, the Cathedral of the Twelve Apostles, a plain white chapel with five silvered domes, adjoins the 17th-century Patriarch Nikon's palace. Together they house the Museum of 17th- and 18th-century Russian Applied Art and Life, including work in precious metals, embroidery, icons and illuminated books.

Armoury

Begun in the 16th century as weapons workshops, these palatial buildings *(Oruzheynaya Palata)* developed into a centre for Russian arts and crafts, employing the most-talented jewellers, icon-painters, printers, leatherworkers and embroiderers. Later used as a store for church and state treasures, the Armoury became a museum after the Bolshevik revolution.

One of many highlights is the gallery of royal regalia and thrones, including that of Ivan the Terrible and the twin throne of the young Peter I (the Great) and his brother Ivan V. A roomful of coaches stars the luxurious royal carriages used to make the long journey between Moscow and St Petersburg and some beautifully decorated sleighs.

In the same building, the Diamond Fund Exhibition *(Vystavka Almaznogo Fonda)* comprises a collection of precious stones and jewellery that once adorned various tsars and empresses. (Visible only on pre-booked group tours.)

Senate

If you're expecting to see the President and other government figures, you're likely to be disap-

pointed. Their offices are in the triangular Senate building, near the northeast wall, topped by a large green dome, and the former headquarters of the Supreme Soviet nearby.

Around Red Square

The first expansion of the city beyond the Kremlin formed an arc around it on the northeast side, centred on the great open space known as Red Square *(Krasnaya Ploshchad)*. Many historic sights, shops and international hotels are within walking distance, though the middle of the square itself is often closed off.

Red Square

The name has nothing to do with the former communist regime, nor with the colours of its buildings: it results from the shared derivation of the words "beautiful" *(krasivaya)* and "red" *(krasnaya)*. Thus in the 16th century it meant "beautiful square". A meeting place, market and parade ground, the square was famous in Soviet times for vast displays of military might, processions of tanks and missiles, troops and Young Pioneers waving to the party bosses assembled on the roof of Lenin's Tomb.

The colourful interior of St Basil's Cathedral.

St Basil's Cathedral

If one building has come to symbolize Moscow, it is this fantasy of colour, twisting shapes and "oriental" style (the inspiration is in fact Russian, taking the onion domes of early wooden churches to the ultimate). *Sobor Vasilia Blazhenogo* was built between 1554–61 to celebrate Ivan the Terrible's victory over the Tatar khans of Kazan. The story that he had the architects blinded to prevent them creating anything more beautiful is certainly a myth.

Under each dome is a chapel. There were originally nine, but another was added in 1588, over the grave of St Basil, who had forecast Ivan's eternal damnation. Parts of the interior are still under restoration, but early frescoes can be seen, and some areas are used for exhibitions. The statue in front of the cathedral is of Minin and Pozharsky, who led the forces that threw the Polish army out of Moscow in 1612. The stone platform nearby was once the site of public executions.

An incongruous backdrop to St Basil's, the massive Hotel Rossiya was the world's biggest when it opened in the 1970s. Guests complained that it took ten minutes to find their rooms.

Lenin's Tomb

Against his and his widow's wishes, Lenin's body was em- 25

balmed when he died in 1924 and put on display, first in a temporary structure, then in this red and black granite blockhouse (*Mavzoley Lenina*) next to the Kremlin Wall. It still attracts a procession of visitors, though not as many as in Soviet days when the line stretched out of sight. (The opening hours and rate of admission were regulated to keep it impressively long.) Access is by way of a security gate next to the State History Museum.

Stalin's body joined that of Lenin in 1953, but in 1961, after Khrushchev's denunciation of the tyrant, delegates to the party congress proposed that it should be removed. One actually declared that Lenin himself had appeared to her in a vision to say that he did not wish to share his place of rest with Comrade Stalin (and nobody laughed). Stalin was duly taken out and buried next to the Kremlin wall. After the fall of communism there were calls for Lenin to be given the same treatment (even for a "Christian burial"). Yet, at the time of writing, he remains in place, a bizarre icon to the faithful and the curious. Visitors, instructed by the guards to keep quiet and remove their hats, descend the stairs to a darkened chamber. Only the corpse is illuminated, behind glass. Its waxen face is the result of embalming and restorations.

Graves and Memorials

Plaques in the Kremlin wall behind the tomb, and graves in the garden nearby, commemorate various Soviet heroes: Yuri Gagarin, the first cosmonaut; Marshal Zhukov the defender of Stalingrad; several of Stalin's henchmen, and the old tyrant himself; later Soviet leaders including Brezhnev, Andropov and Chernenko, and Igor Kurchatov, father of the Soviet H-bomb. One of the rare foreigners to be honoured is John Reed (*Dzhon Rid*), the American journalist and author of *Ten Days that Shook the World*, a rose-coloured view of the Bolshevik revolution published in 1920.

GUM

The name is an acronym, from the Russian for State Universal Store (*Gosudarstvenniy Universalniy Magazin*); the splendid 19th-century building takes up most of the northwest side of Red Square. When it first opened, it housed hundreds of little shops selling everything under the sun. Under Soviet government ownership it was renowned for long queues, shabby goods or empty shelves. Now privatized, its attractive boutiques are full of foreign luxuries, Russian crafts, fur hats and electronic equipment, the widest choice to be found in the capital.

The pride of Moscow is also the quickest and cheapest way to get around. You need a bilingual map, and it helps if you can read the station names in the Cyrillic alphabet—though in the cars themselves they are given in both Cyrillic and latin letters. Note that *Vkhod* means Entrance, *Vykhod v gorod* is Exit to City and *Perekhod* means the walkway to another line.

The layout is like the spokes of a wheel, with a circle line roughly following the Garden Ring. Buy a token for each journey, to travel an unlimited distance on the fast, frequent trains. As well as the trip, you get to see the amazing stations. More like palaces or museums, some are filled with heroic statues, some lined with mosaics, paintings or reliefs. Stained glass at Novoslobodskaya, allegorical sculptures at Ploshchad Revolyutsii, marble and chandeliers at Mayakovskaya, Ukrainian history at Kievskaya and statues of war heroes at Komsomolskaya are some striking examples—just get off at a few stations to find more. The system is not quite as spotless as in Soviet times and advertisements are now permitted to sully these temples to the revolution—the Marxist revolution.

Kazan Cathedral

The church that stood in the north corner of Red Square, built in 1636, was razed to the ground 300 years later to make way for Stalin's huge parades. With the religious revival in 1991 came a decision to rebuild it; by 1993 the replica was complete. It's a pretty sight in pink, green and white, with gilded helmet-shaped dome, light interior, bright iconostasis and colourful frescoes, and a constant stream of worshippers.

State History Museum

At the northwestern end of Red Square stands a red-brick building whose silvery-white roof looks as if it's covered in snow. The *Istorichesky Muzey* opened in 1883, its elaborate rooms filled with vast collections from Stone Age tools to tsarist times, and special exhibitions such as coins and court dress. Labelling is in Russian and English.

Manezh Square

Behind the History Museum, an equestrian statue honours Marshal Georgi Zhukov, nemesis of the Nazis. It stands out against a dome and kitschy fountain dripping with grotesque statues of fairy-tale characters, flanked by escalators leading underground to the country's largest shopping centre. The ensemble was inaugurated in 1997 to celebrate the city's 850th anniversary. On the south side of the square, the huge neoclassical Manezh (riding school) or Central Exhibition Hall was burnt to the ground on March 14, 2004, leaving only the outer shell.

Bolshoy Theatre

Facing Theatre Square (*Teatralnaya Ploschad*), the world-famous Bolshoy, with its plush red and gold auditorium and tiers of balconies and boxes, has stood here since the end of the 18th century. It is now undergoing renovation, and performances are given in a new, temporary building next door.

At any given time, at least one Bolshoy ballet company is likely to be touring the world in pursuit of foreign currency, but there are more than enough dancers to stage the standard items of the repertoire. Ballet alternates with opera, and although some performances are rather perfunctory, there are memorable exceptions.

Moscow Chekhov Art Theatre

Founded by the director Stanislavsky in 1898, the Moscow Art Theatre introduced Chekhov to the world—the premiere of *Uncle Vanya* was staged here in 1899. Mikhail Gorbachev said that a performance of the same play in 1987 persuaded him of the sickness of Soviet society and the need for "major surgery". The theatre, a short walk west of Theatre Square, still puts on classics by Pushkin, Chekhov and the once-banned Bulgakov.

Tverskaya Street

The former Gorky Street is Moscow's liveliest thoroughfare, with bright modern shops, new hotels, restaurants and clubs, most of them far beyond the means of the average Muscovite but a magnet to the rich "New Russians".

Just north of Pushkin Square, the former Revolution Museum, now the Museum of Modern History *(Muzey sovremennoy istorii)* occupies a lovely old palace. It used to romanticize the 1917 revolution and the achievements of the Soviet state, but since 1991 it has tried to give a more balanced and honest view. There are accounts of life in the Siberian Gulag "archipelago" (Solzhenitsyn's word for the labour camps scattered like islands amid the forests and snowfields), and the campaigns against the church, the *kulaks* (better-off peasants) and other class enemies. Displays cover environmental pollution and the Chernobyl nuclear disaster. Former non-persons, expunged from the record at various times in the past, have made a reappearance, from Nicholas II and his family, Trotsky and Bukharin to the master of rewritten history, Stalin. Labelling is only in Russian but the evocative old photographs speak volumes.

Lubyanka Square

The former Dzerzhinsky Square, named after the founder of the USSR's secret police, has reverted to its older but still sinister name, that of the notorious KGB headquarters and prison which faces it. The KGB's less frightening successor, the State Security Service (FSB), now uses the red and grey fortress. In bizarre contrast, the Children's World *(Dyetsky Mir)* department store also looks on to the square.

Central Moscow – West and South

Two historic monasteries, two magnificent art collections and a host of other attractions are scattered on both sides of the Moskva river as it makes a great double bend south of the Kremlin.

Arbat District

Many old houses survive in the streets around Arbat Square, where Novy Arbat crosses the Boulevard Ring. Heading away from the square, Novy Arbat is lined by apartment and government buildings perched on top of a two-storey shopping and entertainment complex. Much of old Moscow was razed in the 1960s to make way for this vision of a 29 socialist future, which looks a lot less appealing than the little shops it replaced. Old Arbat Street, the left fork at Arbat Square, is a pedestrian zone, and the weekend focus of art shows, impromptu concerts and market stalls.

White House

Where Novy Arbat Street meets the Moskva river, the White House *(Bely dom)* was the seat of the Russian parliament and scene of two historic confrontations. In 1991, Boris Yeltsin as newly elected President of Russia persuaded army units surrounding it to change sides and support him.

STALIN'S WEDDING CAKES

The University building is one of a handful of ornate towers built in the 1950s to show that Moscow could rival New York in reaching for the sky. Others are the Ukraine Hotel across the Moskva river from the White House, the Ministry of Foreign Affairs and a couple of apartment blocks. The only export model is a monumental eyesore planted in the middle of Warsaw. Stylistically they were 20 years out of date, and maintenance has always been a problem. Expensive plans are sometimes announced for their refurbishment, and then deferred indefinitely.

30

In 1993, he ordered tanks to fire on the building when it was occupied by defiant opponents trying to unseat him.

Victory Park

Kutuzovsky Prospekt continues the line and style of Novy Arbat for several kilometres, past a triumphal arch commemorating the victory over Napoleon and a pavilion with a huge 360° panoramic painting of the Battle of Borodino. Beyond this is the park, opened in 1995 to mark the 50th anniversary of the victorious end to the Great Patriotic War, with monuments, statues, guns, tanks and vistas. On weekends, Moscow's youth gather to roller-blade or dance to deafening sound systems.

Pushkin Fine Arts Museum

A white marble palace near the southwest corner of the Kremlin houses Moscow's major museum of world art *(Muzey Izobrazitelnykh Iskusstv Imeni Pushkina)*. If you are short of time you could miss the ancient Egyptian, Greek and Roman sculptures and concentrate on the Western European art. Tsars, aristocrats and rich merchants contributed—mostly involuntarily—to the marvellous collection. In recent years, the museum has admitted to having many masterpieces that were seized in Germany at the end of

World War II, works that had previously been looted by the Nazis. Some have been displayed in special shows; negotiations for their possible return to their original owners' descendants are stalled.

The Spanish School includes pictures by El Greco and Murillo, the Italian has works of Botticelli and Veronese. There are several by Rembrandt and many by other Dutch masters; the French collection stars Poussin, Watteau, David, Delacroix and Corot. Most stunning of all are the four galleries of Impressionists and post-Impressionists, with all the famous names represented by works of the highest quality. Monet, Renoir, Cézanne, Gauguin, Van Gogh (*The Red Vineyards*) and Degas hang in thrilling profusion. Early Picassos include *Girl on a Ball* and there's a whole wall of Matisse.

Cathedral of Christ the Saviour

The enormous white church (*Khram Khrista Spasitelya*), with reddish-gold fluted domes across the street and a short way south of the Pushkin Museum, looks old but new. That's because the 19th-century original was knocked down on Stalin's orders in 1931, and a swimming pool built in its place. This is a replica, paid for in part by the gifts of the faithful and built after the fall of communism. Construction was completed in 1997, to mark the 850th anniversary of the founding of Moscow. Nicholas II and his family were canonized here in 2000 by the Patriarch Alexis II.

Novodevichy Convent

Southwest of the Kremlin, protected by a loop of the Moskva river, is a smaller "walled city" of haunting beauty. Behind high battlements and a dozen watchtowers, its domes and pinnacles and a great six-tiered belfry look like the illustrations from a Russian fairy tale. The convent, founded in the 16th century, saw Boris Godunov proclaimed tsar in 1598. Peter the Great imprisoned his half-sister Sophia here, and later his first wife, on suspicion of conspiring against him.

The most impressive building is the Smolensk Cathedral (1525), with five cupolas and a bell tower added in 1690. The interior is rich with original frescoes and a glowing iconostasis dating from the late 17th century. In 1997, the religious life of the convent was revived when 20 nuns moved in.

In the cemetery, reached by a separate entrance, are the graves of writers Gogol and Chekhov, composers Prokofiev and Shostakovich, film-maker Eisenstein and several Soviet leaders including Molotov and Khrushchev.

31

Rousing performances of music and dance by the Red Army Choir are not to be missed.

Moscow State University

The 32-storey skyscraper topped by a spire, on a hill across the river from Novodevichy, is part of Moscow University. The balustrade at its base is a good viewpoint over the city and a traditional place for wedding parties to come, though these days it is lined by souvenir stalls. Long called after Lenin, these heights have reverted to the charming old name of Sparrow Hills.

Tretyakov Gallery

In the *Tretyakovskaya Galereya*, Moscow possesses the world's finest display of Russian art, from early icons to the 1920s. The two Tretyakov brothers, rich industrialists, gave their own collections to the city in 1892 and paid for the original building, a fairy-tale medieval castle just across the river to the south of the Kremlin. After the Bolshevik revolution, confiscated church and private property boosted the collection.

Icons are in the ground floor rooms. The earliest examples, from the 12th century, include the revered *Mother of God* from Vladimir. It was brought to Moscow in 1390 and hung in the Assumption Cathedral until 1930. Andrey Rublyov's 15th-century *Holy Trinity* comes from Sergiev Posad monastery. More icons can be seen in the Church of St Nicholas, in the gallery's grounds.

In the 18th century, painters began to turn from religious subjects to portraiture, as witness the delightful character studies by Borovikovsky and Levitsky. The 19th century saw artists widening their scope still further, painting rural scenes and peasant life as well as aristocrats and historical tableaux. Among the great names are Perov, Repin (*Ivan the Terrible with the Body of his Son Ivan, Religious Procession in Kursk*), Vrubel with an entire room of his wild mysticism, and Levitan, painter of striking landscapes.

From the early 20th century come Larionov and Goncharova, who designed for Diaghilev's ballets, Cubists including Tatlin, and other leaders of the avant-garde such as Malevich, Klyun and Popova. Many of these works were collected quietly by George Costakis, a Russian citizen of Greek origin who worked for the Canadian embassy for many years. He then donated a large number to the Tretyakov Gallery, in exchange for the right to take some of his favourite pieces abroad.

Only a small part of the museum's wealth can be displayed. This used to be the excuse for not showing anything too controversial, which meant abstract and "modern" art and the work of those such as Chagall and Kandinsky, who had left Russia at the time of the 1917 Revolution. Now the Cubists, Suprematists, Constructivists and others who launched their own revolution in art are honoured, while the pedestrian "Socialist Realism" has been banished to the New Tretyakov near the Moskva river.

Gorky Park

The city's oldest public recreation park lies along the Moskva river upstream from the Kremlin. Immensely popular with Muscovites, it has ornamental gardens, cafés, roller coasters and other fairground attractions, concert stages, a beer hall and boating lake (frozen in winter, it becomes a skating rink). You can view the city from the top of the Big Wheel, listen to live music, and treat yourself to fried chicken and ice cream.

Donskoy Monastery

Several fortress-monasteries were founded over the centuries to defend the approaches to Moscow; this one, near the Moskva river 5 km (3 miles) to the south of the Kremlin, was the last to be built. It stands on the site of a victory over the Tatars in 1591, and was begun in that year. The stone wall with twelve towers dates from about 1700. After the 1917 revo-

33

lution it continued to function (a rarity in the USSR), and became the seat of the Patriarch until it was closed in 1927 and fell into disrepair. Now restored, its churches are again active. The biggest of them all, the brick New Cathedral completed in 1693, has kept its original, finely carved iconostasis.

Kolomenskoye

On the banks of the Moskva river about 10 km (6 miles) southeast of the city centre stands one of the finest collections of early Russian buildings, now designated as an architectural museum. A former large estate of the tsars, it was the site of a vast wooden palace built in the 1660s for Tsar Alexis, and razed a century later by Catherine II.

Kolomenskoye can be reached by Metro, or by river bus on summer weekends. The entrance is through the Spassky Gate; this and the tall white five-domed Kazan church date from Alexis' time. Dotted about the estate are buildings brought from other places and reassembled here: a 17th-century wooden tower from the shores of the White Sea, Peter the Great's wooden cabin from Arkhangelsk and many more. The 1532 Church of the Ascension was the first brick and stone version of a traditional tent-shaped Russian church.

Outskirts – North and East

Former princely estates and royal hunting grounds provide Moscow with plenty of parks. Ostankino is reached by way of the wide Prospekt Mira or a few stops on the Metro. Ismailovsky Park, to the east, is the city's biggest playground.

All-Russia Exhibition Centre

Grandiose statuary and 70 elaborate pavilions mark the site of the former USSR Exhibition of Economic Achievements (VDNKh), which was closed down in 1990 when it became clear that the economy was close to collapse. Now the buildings are used as commercial showrooms and hundreds of market stalls cover the area near the Metro station, still called VDNKh.

A rocket tops the Cosmonauts' Memorial, a titanium arc reaching to a height of 100 m (330 ft). A small space museum is housed in its base.

The curving multi-storey Cosmos Hotel is another landmark, built to accommodate visitors to the 1980 Olympic Games.

Ostankino

Moscow's TV tower stands on the southern edge of Ostankino Park, once the summer estate of the immensely rich Sheremetyev family. The tower has a glass-

34

enclosed viewing platform at 330 m (1,080 ft) providing the best panorama of the city.

To the north is the pink and white palace in neoclassical style with a great portico, built in 1792–97 by the serfs of Count Sheremetyev—superb artisans, to judge by the carving, plasterwork, parquet floors and furniture. It's hard to believe, but the construction is entirely of wood, stuccoed to look like stone. The largest room in the house is the theatre, with an ingenious mechanism to remove the seats and turn it into a ballroom. The count had a passion for the theatre and kept a company of serf-actors to put on plays.

Near the palace, Trinity Church (1678) is an elaborate fantasy of brick, stone columns, round gables and multiple onion domes topped with crosses.

Ismailovsky Park

Once the tsars' hunting ground, this is Moscow's biggest area of parkland and forest, 10 km (6 miles) east of the centre. A large Soviet-era hotel plays host to many tour groups. The western end near the Park Metro station has cafés, play areas, a massive wholesale market and a weekend market with craft stalls and artists selling their paintings. In the eastern part, shaded paths wind through vast tracts of pine woods.

Kuskovo

Like Ostankino, Kuskovo, 12 km (7 miles) east of the city, was an estates of the Sheremetyev family. It too has a stuccoed wooden classical palace; operas are sometimes staged in its lovely White Hall. The buildings in the French-style formal gardens include a palatial 18th-century baroque grotto, a little red Dutch House (1749) lined with Delft tiles and an Orangery, now used as a museum of ceramics.

RIVER BUSES

In summer, motor boats and hydrofoils operate ferry services along the Moskva river and connecting canals. Boarding points include Gorky Park and the Kievsky railway station, where three Metro lines also converge. Bargain-priced sightseeing cruises, lasting about an hour and a half, start from landing stages near the Kremlin.

From land or water, you can't miss the huge statue of Peter the Great, standing before the mast of a tall ship, upstream from the Kremlin where the river and canal divide. It was paid for by a private donor and put up in 1996, amid great controversy; since Peter disliked Moscow and the feeling was mutual, some said it should be in St Petersburg.

35

Day trips out of the city can be made to some former estates of the aristocracy, but if you can only take one excursion it should be to the Trinity Monastery of St Sergius at Sergiev Posad, one of the historic cities of the Golden Ring and an important religious site.

Arkhangelskoye

The princely Yusupov family used to spend their summers at this smaller version of Versailles, 22 km (14 miles) west of Moscow. The late 18th-century palace awaits restoration, but it is usually possible to visit the elaborate Italianate gardens with their classical statuary (and one of Pushkin). Also in the grounds is a theatre where the Yusupovs' private company of serf-actors performed. Pre-dating any of the estate buildings is the charming white-painted Church of the Archangel Michael (1667).

Abramtsevo

In the mid-19th century, the Abramtsevo estate 60 km (37 miles) northeast of Moscow was the home of Sergey Axakov, a pioneer of Russian realism, and a favourite retreat of writers including Turgenev and Gogol. The industrialist Savva Mamontov, patron of artists, composers and singers, bought it in the 1870s and turned it into an artists' colony. Repin, Levitan, Vrubel and Serov were among those who painted in these peaceful surroundings.

In the main house of what is called the Abramtsevo Estate Museum-Preserve, you can see rooms as they were furnished in the days of Axakov and Mamontov. A small church in the old Russian style has icons by Repin, and a fanciful "Hut on Chicken Legs" recalls a favourite Russian folk tale about the witch Baba Yaga.

Sergiev Posad

The blue and gold cupolas of the Trinity Monastery of St Sergius (*Troitse Sergieva Lavra*) mark one of the most celebrated centres of the Russian Orthodox Church. As the seat of the patriarchate, it was permitted to function even during the Soviet era, when the town was known as Zagorsk. Now the patriarch has moved to the Danilovsky Monastery in Moscow, but there is an active seminary, and pilgrims come from all over Russia and beyond.

The monastery was founded by St Sergius in 1340 and became one of the richest in Russia, thanks to the patronage of tsars,

A clutch of dachas near Sergiev Posad – weekend or summer homes for city-dwellers.

nobles and merchants. Its massive outer wall, 1,370 m (4,500 ft) long, has 11 towers; you enter through the imposing main gate, itself crowned by the Church of St John the Baptist. Within the holy enclosure are several more churches, including the Church of the Assumption (1585), with a central gold dome and four blue ones embellished with gold stars. It is used for services in the summer, but visitors can enter, and may be lucky enough to hear the choir, said to be the best in Russia. The tomb of Boris Godunov, the only tsar buried neither in the Kremlin nor in St Petersburg, stands outside the west door.

The smaller Trinity Cathedral, built in the early 15th century, houses the tomb of St Sergius. Lit only by candles and oil lamps, its many icons include masterpieces by Rublyov and his school.

The eye-catching building with walls in a patchwork design of painted triangles is the former pilgrims' refectory, dating from about 1690, with St Sergius Church at one end. Its iconostasis, a glowing creation of gilding, carving and painting, is not the original, but one saved from the Moscow Church of St Nicholas the Miracleworker, which was razed in 1930 to build a Metro station.

37

◗ THE GOLDEN RING
Vladimir, Suzdal, Yaroslavl, Kostroma, Rostov-Veliky, Pereslavl-Zalessky

The historic towns spread in an arc between Moscow and the Volga, with their picturesque old churches and walled monasteries, are the basis of a fascinating tour. It needs several days; a week would be ideal. Suzdal and Kostroma have hotels of a reasonable standard.

Vladimir

An industrial town on the main road about 190 km (118 miles) east of Moscow, Vladimir has its share of grim-looking factories and apartment blocks, but the historic centre has been marvellously preserved, almost unscarred by the 20th century. It was fortified by the Kievan ruler Vladimir Monomakh in the 12th century to defend his lands. His grandson Andrey Bogolyubsky ("loved by God") made it the capital, but power gradually shifted to Moscow which proved more adept at dealing with the Tatars.

The mid-12th-century Cathedral of the Assumption was the model for its namesake in the Moscow Kremlin; with its golden cupolas, it dominates the town from the high ground above the Klyazma River. Its most sacred treasure, the 11th- or 12th-century icon of the Virgin and Child known as the *Mother of God* was moved to Moscow in 1390. (It is now in the Tretyakov Gallery.) An early 15th-century icon and frescoes by Rublyov can still be seen.

Nearby is the Cathedral of St Dmitry, built in 1194–97 of white stone with a single dome. Originally square with three apses, it was enclosed in the present outer wall soon afterwards. A wealth of stone carving around the main door and on all four walls shows scenes scarcely related to Christian beliefs, with Alexander the Great on the south wall and the Labours of Hercules on the west. King David enchants the animals and birds with his music on the upper north, west and south sides.

The Golden Gate of Vladimir, in the largely vanished western wall, was modelled on the Great Gate of Kiev. It now houses a museum of military history. Next to it is the brick Old Believers' Church (1913), now a museum of miniature painting and glass. The white stone tomb of Alexander Nevsky lies in the Nativity Monastery on the south side of the

Sleigh ride in the snow past Suzdal's Nativity Cathedral.

main street, but his remains were moved to St Petersburg by Peter the Great.

Bogolyubovo

Andrey Bogolyubsky built a fortified palace where the Klyazma and Nerl rivers meet, 12 km (7 miles) east of Vladimir. Little more than one tower and part of a gallery remains of that building, adjoining a 19th-century monastery (now an active convent again) and next to the Assumption Cathedral.

East of the village, reached by walking through meadows where you may hear quail and corncrake calling among the wild flowers, you can find the lovely little Church of the Intercession on the Nerl river. Tall, square, of subtly carved white stone, it also dates from the time of Prince Andrey, though the dome is a 19th-century addition.

Suzdal

Now a lovely, tranquil village of little wooden houses and vegetable gardens, Suzdal was once the capital of the region, and became a major centre of pilgrimage from the 16th to the 18th centuries. Most of its 36 churches, its many monasteries and fine houses for the clergy were built in that period although a few are much older. They now form one of the world's richest assemblies

of religious architecture. Because the railway came no nearer than Vladimir, 40 km (25 miles) to the south, it was never touched by the industrial age.

A low earthen rampart is all that remains of the 12th-century kremlin wall, almost enclosed by a great loop of the Kamenka river as it flows through water meadows. Blue domes scattered with gold stars crown the Nativity of the Virgin Cathedral (Rozhdestvensky Sobor) in the middle of the kremlin. First completed in 1230, it was partly destroyed in Tatar raids and rebuilt in the 16th century. The carved white stone of the lower walls marks the early work; the brick upper levels were added in the restoration, the domes in the 18th century. Frescoes, some of them 13th-century originals, adorn the gorgeous interior. The cathedral's ancient oak doors—the Golden Gates—are decorated with gilded copper sheets engraved with biblical scenes.

On the south side of the cathedral courtyard, the archbishop's palace houses a museum of history and religious art. Its collection of icons includes the 13th-century Holy Virgin of Maximovska. To the south, the wooden St Nicholas Church was built in 1766 without the use of nails.

Across the river, the open-air Museum of Wooden Architecture

Huts on stilts by the Kamenka River are used for storing hay.

and Peasant Life includes fully furnished houses, windmills and a man-powered wheel to pump water from a well.

At the northern end of town, the walled Intercession Convent *(Pokrovsky Monastyr)* was used for some years as a hotel, with new log cabins in the grounds, but it is now back in the hands of the church. On the other side of the river is the Saviour Monastery of St Euthymius *(Spaso-Yev-fimievsky Monastyr),* Suzdal's largest. Behind its high brick walls stand the seven-domed 16th-century Cathedral of the Transfiguration, its separate bell tower and three more churches.

After the 1917 revolution the compound was used as a prison, first for political prisoners, then for the German generals captured at Stalingrad, and until 1970 for convicted prostitutes.

Yaroslavl

Founded in 1010 by Yaroslav the Wise of Kiev, the city now has a population of 750,000, a vast oil refinery and diesel engine factory. It stretches along both banks of the Volga for about 30 km (18 miles).

The historic heart stands 70 m (230 ft) above the river where it is joined by the Kotorosl river. The white-walled Monastery of the 41

Transfiguration of the Saviour *(Spaso-Preobrazhensky Monastyr)* was founded in the 12th century, although the cathedral and gates date mainly from the 16th, when this was the richest and most imposing fortress-monastery on the Volga. The bell tower was given a 19th-century top.

The five-domed Church of Elijah *(Tserkov Ilyi Proroka)* on the main square, built in the 17th century, has its original iconostasis and brilliantly painted frescoes of Old Testament scenes. Old markets, trading arcades and fine merchants' houses, art museums and Russia's oldest surviving theatre attest to the former prosperity of a river port and city that once rivalled Moscow.

Kostroma

Until 1990, Kostroma's military installations kept it off limits to foreign visitors. In spite of its size and population of 350,000, it hardly appeared on Soviet maps. Standing beside the Volga, 90 km (55 miles) downriver from Yaroslavl, it's surrounded by vast tracts of forest, and still has many wooden houses. After near-total destruction in a great fire in 1773, the old centre was rebuilt in the classical style of the time. The story goes that Catherine II, dissatisfied with the plans she had been shown, threw her open fan on the table and said: "Build it like that!" And indeed, the street pattern is fan-shaped, focusing on Susanin Square.

Fortunately the marvellous Monastery of St Ipaty *(Ipatevsky Monastyr),* across the Kostroma river where it meets the Volga, escaped the fire. It was founded in the 14th century by the ancestors of Boris Godunov, and became a place of exile for his rivals the Romanovs. Mikhail Romanov was living here when emissaries came in 1613 to beg him to accept the throne and put an end to the Time of Troubles, and for the next three centuries almost every Romanov tsar came on a kind of pilgrimage. The gold-domed Trinity Cathedral *(Troitsky Sobor)* built around 1600 has a superb iconostasis of gold and carved wood, and early frescoes by the Kostroma school of painters led by Yuri Nikitin. The old mansion where the Romanovs lived now houses an exhibition about the last tsar Nicholas II and his family, with many old photographs, letters and watercolours painted by his children. In a walled compound next to the monastery, the 1712 wooden Church of the Transfiguration is a rarity, standing on 24 stilts to keep it clear of floods on its former site. It was moved here in 1961.

Next to the main road-bridge over the Volga stands the highly decorated 17th-century Church of the Resurrection *(Tserkov Voskresenia)*, built by a rich merchant. It's said that he paid for it with a barrel of gold coins sent from England by mistake instead of the indigo dye that he had ordered. The church has a revered 13th-century icon to which foreign princesses prayed before marrying into the Russian royal family, when they were expected to adopt the Orthodox faith and take a Russian name. Imperial double eagles in the decoration of the church somehow survived the Soviet period.

Rostov-Veliky

Standing beside a lake on the road from Moscow to Yaroslavl, Rostov the Great was founded before either, in the 9th century. Now it's a big, ugly industrial sprawl, but on the very edge its ancient kremlin survives, miraculously unaffected. Its walls and fine gate-towers ring a compound packed with churches dating from about 1690. Just outside the

north wall, the Cathedral of the Assumption *(Uspensky Sobor)* is a century older. Next to it, the tall Church of the Resurrection stands directly over the elaborate North Gate. The whole ensemble is a vision of old Russia as perfect as any on the Golden Ring, and much less visited than Suzdal, Vladimir or Sergiev Posad.

Pereslavl-Zalessky

Northeast of Sergiev Posad on the road to Yaroslav lies an ancient lakeside town founded by Yuri Dolgoruky at about the same time as Moscow. Only a low, grass-covered earth rampart remains to mark the line of its kremlin walls, but scattered churches and monasteries recall its former importance. The little Cathedral of the Transfiguration is one of Russia's oldest churches, begun in the 12th century and restored in the 19th. To the southwest of town is the Goritsky Monastery, with a 17th-century cathedral, superb icons and a museum containing marvels of church decoration.

4

FOUR BEAUTIFUL CHURCHES Unique in their different ways are the little 12th-century **Church of the Intercession**, Bogolyubovo; the carved stone **Cathedral of St Dmitry** in Vladimir; the 22-domed wooden **Church of the Transfiguration** on Kizhi Island in Lake Onega; and Rastrelli's enchanting baroque **Smolny Cathedral** in St Petersburg.

➤ ST PETERSBURG
Peter and Paul Fortress, Vasilyevsky Island,
Around Palace Square, Between the Neva and the
Griboyedov Canal, Nevski Prospekt, From Arts Square
to the Smolny Convent

Like Venice and Amsterdam, St Petersburg is a city on water, laced by rivers and canals, sewn together by hundreds of bridges. The pleasing plan of parks, palaces, boulevards and monuments devised by 18th-century architects has survived wars and revolutions; only gilded spires and domes break the skyline. For decades, the city looked much the worse for wear. Winter has always been an enemy, its allies damp and pollution, all eroding the stucco façades. Every spring saw them in need of cleaning or a coat of paint, but most had to do without, and the shabbiness went unnoticed on the "white nights" of summer when people walk up and down the banks of the Neva all night long. But the city was given a facelift for the tricentenary celebrations in 2003.

Peter and Paul Fortress

Peter the Great's first priority in building his new city was a stronghold to control the river. He chose Zayachy (Hare) Island in the Neva, a short distance from its mouth in the gulf of Finland, as the site of a fortress (*Petropavlovskaya Krepost*). Work began in May 1703. Designed as an irregular hexagon, with walls of wood and mud, to plans drawn up by the tsar himself, it evolved in time into a fully-fledged citadel protected by impressive red-brick and stone ramparts with strategically placed bastions. It still encloses a number of buildings, including the Peter and Paul Cathedral, the Mint, in activity today, the barracks of the former garrison and the gloomy cells of the Trubetskoy bastion prison. At midday, a cannon salutes the raising of the colours. As evening falls, join the crowds strolling beneath the ramparts: the view over the Neva and the palaces on the south bank is magnificent.

Peter and Paul Cathedral

The dominant building within the fortress is the cathedral (*Petropavlovsky sobor*) built in Dutch baroque style between 1712 and 1733 by the Swiss architect Domenico Trezzini. Its

St Petersburg's Russian Museum has a superb collection of icons, an art introduced to Kiev by monks from Byzantium.

45

needle-like spire, covered with gold leaf and topped by an angel bearing a cross, is one of the city's landmarks. It is the city's highest building, 122.5 m (402 ft) tall and is visible from far away. St Petersburg, virtually floating in its marsh, was spared the skyscrapers that were to disfigure Moscow during the Stalin era.

The exterior is otherwise unimpressive, but inside is a different story. Peter is buried in these sumptuous surroundings, together with most of his successors—all the Romanovs except Peter II, interred in the Kremlin. On July 17, 1998, 80 years day for day after their execution at Yekaterinburg, the remains of Tsar Nicholas II, Empress Alexandra, three of their daughters, the family doctor and three servants were buried in St Catherine's chapel, having been retrieved from a mineshaft and authenticated by DNA tests. Note the huge icon screen in gilded wood, affixed to the shrine like a stage curtain. In front stands a cross of mammoth ivory, a replica of the original designed by Peter the Great.

At the exit, you can see an exhibition on the history of Russian coinage.

Trubetskoy Bastion Prison Museum

When the military significance of the fortress diminished, it was used as a place of imprisonment —a role it held for two centuries. Peter the Great's own son Alexis was incarcerated in the dungeons for six months before being tortured to death on the orders of his father. Generations of political prisoners followed, including Dostoyevsky, Gorky and Trotsky. If you visit the row of prison cells, you will see the one where Lenin's elder brother Alexander was detained for two months, a short time before the bolsheviks made the fortress one of their rallying points.

Other Museums

Several rooms of the fortress are used for permanent exhibitions. The most interesting, in the Engineers' House, displays the collections of the Museum of Old St Petersburg: stained-glass windows, porcelain, wrought iron, old photographs and paintings of the city.

The Former Commandant's House, opposite the Arsenal at the back of the cathedral, is devoted to the history of St Petersburg. The Museum of Furniture and Decorative Arts (of the 16th–20th centuries) is open for group tours only. On a completely different subject, the Museum of Space Exploration is located on the site of the first gas-dynamics laboratory where jet propulsion engines were developed.

In the "white nights" of summer, darkness never falls on St Petersburg.

Peter's Cabin

The oldest house in the city *(Domik Petra* is a log cabin quickly erected in 1703 for Peter the Great to live in while the city was being built. It has been venerated ever since, and is preserved in a small, stone-built museum. Measuring only 12 m by 5.5 m (39×18 ft), it consists of three rooms: a large study, with an armchair designed by the tsar himself, a rather rustic dining room and a tiny bedroom.

A short walk from here, the superb Trinity Bridge *(Troickij most)*, designed by Gustave Eiffel, straddles the Neva. You have to cross it to get to the city centre, stopping to admire the lovely views from the parapets.

The Aurora

Further east, not far from Peter's Cabin, is moored the old three-funnelled cruiser *Aurora*, built in 1900 and credited with firing the cannon that signalled the Bolshevik assault on the Winter Palace in 1917. Like that event, the ship's role has been surrounded by myth and legend, tales that are recounted in an exhibition inside this historic monument—including the parts it played in the 1904–05 war between Russia and Japan and in World War II.

47

Vasilyevsky Island

Downriver from the Peter and Paul Fortress, the Neva splits into two branches at the spit of this large island, which stops up the mouth of the delta like a cork. Flanking the square at its eastern tip, called the Strelka, are two monumental red rostral columns, studded with the spurs of ships designed to rip asunder the sides of enemy vessels. At the base of the columns are statues personifying the four great waterways of western Russia—the Dnieper, the Volga, the Volkhov and the Neva. The columns were used in the 19th century as lighthouses to guide boats into the port, the lights provided by burning hemp oil in the bronze bowls at the top. From here there's a splendid view over the river and south bank, with the Winter Palace in the foreground.

Museums

Several museums are grouped in the east part of the island. The former Exchange now houses the Central Naval Museum, where you can see, among others, a boat that belonged to Peter the Great, the "grandfather of the Russian navy". There's a zoology museum, a geology museum, and another devoted to ethnology and anthropology founded on the tsar's cabinet of curiosities (*Kunstkamera*).

Menshikov Palace

Going down the avenue that runs beside the Neva, you pass the University before reaching the Menshikov Palace at no. 15, its walls painted a bright saffron yellow. The oldest stone building in St Petersburg, it was the home of Prince Menshikov, first governor of the city and a close friend of Peter the Great. It soon proved to be more luxurious than the tsar's own Summer Palace, and was occasionally used for state receptions. Part of the interior has been preserved since the 18th century. There is a fine collection of Delft porcelain.

Around Palace Square

No square in Europe is more aristocratic than Dvortsovaya Ploshchad, a vast open space surrounded by superb buildings. The column in the centre, at 47 m (154 ft) the tallest of its kind, commemorates Russia's victory over Napoleon's army in 1812. On the south side is one of those rare architectural achievements that combine great mass and beauty. Its two parts, linked by a double triumphal arch four storeys high and topped by the Chariot of Victory, were built in the 1830s to serve as the headquarters of the army General Staff and the Ministry of Foreign Affairs. The architect, Carlo Rossi, a Russian of Italian origin, believed in thinking big. Its concave façade, 600 m (nearly 2,000 ft) in length, is painted in a rich yellow with white trim that looks as well against winter snow as in the endless golden evenings of midsummer.

This square has a special place in the heart of the inhabitants, being the site of many demonstrations and revolts. In January 1905, on "Bloody Sunday", the troops fired on the crowds of workers come to claim food from the tsar, triggering off the first Russian revolution. In this same square, Lenin led the Bolsheviks to power in 1917. And in 1991, during the conservative Communists' attempt at a coup d'Etat, more than 100,000 citizens gathered here to claim democracy.

Winter Palace
A seemingly endless baroque palace (Zimny Dvorets), painted pale green with decorative features picked out in white and gold, faces the river on one side and Palace Square on the other. Built as the royal winter quarters between 1754 and 1762, it was the greatest achievement of Count Bartolomeo Rastrelli, the son of a Florentine sculptor who became the favourite architect of Empress Elizabeth. The main residence of the imperial court for more than 150 years, the palace flourished under Catherine II, who was the first to really live there. The interiors, largely destroyed by a fire in 1837, were revamped in a neoclassical style, apart from the grand staircase which remained unchanged. Improvising with painted stucco for lack of local stone, Rastrelli added columns and pilasters, statues and complex arched windows. The interplay of all this relief with the low, slanting northern light creates a stunning effect, part-central European, part-Russian and unique to St Petersburg.

Hermitage Museum
The eastern extension of the Winter Palace, the Hermitage was built as a retreat for Catherine II, and some of her growing art collection was kept here. Nicholas I added to the building and opened part of it as a museum in 1852. After the 1917 revolution it was expanded when some large private collections were confiscated (the Moscow merchant Shchukin involuntarily donated 27 paintings by Matisse and 31 by Picasso). Although it retained the Hermitage name, the museum overflowed into large parts of the Winter Palace. The Soviet government sold some pictures to Western museums and millionaires in the 1920s to raise money, but the gaps go unnoticed amid such riches.

49

Visitors to the Hermitage dwarfed by the opulent magnificence of the Ambassadors' Staircase.

There's no other museum like the Hermitage; it is immense, with over 350 rooms and 3 million works of art! It is quite impossible to see everything in a day, even in two. You can buy a ticket and go in on your own, but a better plan—though it's quite expensive—is to take a guided tour first to get an idea of the layout. Tours are offered in various languages by hotels, travel agencies and the Hermitage itself, and, in summer, have the advantage of bypassing any waiting lines. When the tour ends, you can stay in and wander at leisure to explore further the sections that interest you most. Another

solution is to hire an audioguide, which are well produced and available in several languages. The entrance is on the river side.

More than a museum, the Hermitage is first and foremost a palace. In the course of your visit, you will discover a succession of richly decorated rooms, reflecting the lifestyle and eclectic tastes of the imperial regime. After the grand staircase, you will see the state rooms, including the Armorial Hall, almost 1000 sq m, enclosed by a cohort of gilded Corinthian columns, and St George's Hall, with the imperial throne at one end. The parquet is made up of 16 different kinds of woods, repeating the same design as the ceiling. The splendid Pavilion Hall was the favourite room of Catherine II; she received her close family and friends beneath the tinkling crystal chandeliers. On one side it looks out over the Neva, and on the other over the hanging garden. Don't miss the spectacular Malachite Room, adorned with 2 tons of the semi-precious green stone, the 1812 Gallery, the Boudoir in crimson and gold, and the elegant Moorish Hall.

Tours speed past some of the star exhibits by the world's greatest painters and sculptors, some of whom fill entire rooms—Rembrandt, Rubens, Van Dyck and other Dutch and Flemish artists. All of western European art is represented: the German school (superb works by Cranach the Elder), Spanish (Velázquez, Goya), French, British and especially Italian (Raphael's *Madonna*, painted at the age of 17, Leonardo da Vinci's *Madonna Litta*, Michelangelo's *Crouching Boy*, marble sculptures by Canova, and so on). On the second floor is an exceptional collection of great French painters from the Impressionists to Picasso. Works by Gauguin, Matisse (the famous *Danse* and *Musique* commissioned by a wealthy Moscow collector) and Van Gogh can be seen alongside others by Cézanne, Derain, Monet, Vuillard, Vlaminck and more. On the ground floor are the ancient Scythian, Egyptian, Greek, Roman, Indian and oriental collections that would each fill large museums of their own.

Pushkin House Museum

To the east of Palace Square, one of the most picturesque sections of the Moyka Canal winds through the centre of the city. Here its banks are lined with colourful palaces. No. 12 Reyki Moyki quay is the last home of the poet Alexander Pushkin, now a museum. It was here that he died, in 1837, after a duel with a French soldier. In the rooms overlooking the river, in his study, a few souvenirs have been gathered together: his pen, his pipe, his books and his death mask.

Between the Neva and the Griboyedov Canal

West of Palace Square, beside the Neva, stretches the building around which Peter the Great planned his town: the Admiralty. There are several other sights of interest further south along the banks of the Moyka and beyond, beside the Kriukov canal.

The Admiralty

Peter the Great founded a naval shipyard just to the west of the 51

Winter Palace in 1704. The Admiralty building that took over the site a century later is a majestic neoclassical landmark and symbol of the city, its golden spire surmounting a square tower enclosed in a classical colonnade, all supported by a massive arch painted yellow and white. The spire, 73 m (239 ft) high, is topped by a weathervane shaped like a caravel. The portals and columns, statues and friezes of mermaids and tritons all celebrate the city's vigour and former maritime importance. Today the Admiralty is still home to a Russian naval college.

Decembrists' Square

The open space just to the west of the Admiralty, *Ploschad Dekabristov,* is named in honour of the revolutionaries who gathered here

in the failed coup of December 1825. Some of the perpetrators were condemned to death but most of them exiled to Siberia. *The Bronze Horseman*, Etienne Falconet's statue of Peter the Great on horseback, stands between the square and the river, near the Alexander garden. As an inscription on its massive stone base declares, it is Catherine the Great's tribute to Peter I, erected in 1782.

Pushkin's last home was on the Moyka Canal, where he died after a duel with a French soldier.

St Isaac's Cathedral

To the south of the square, St Isaac's *(Isaakievsky Sobor)* was completed in 1858 after 40 years of labour. It took more than 100 kg of gold leaf to cover the dome. This was the last neoclassical edifice to be built in St Petersburg. Each of its four identical façades is composed of a wide pediment supported by huge Corinthian columns, each one weighing 114 tons! The granite used in their construction was brought from Finland on barges and in carts specially designed for the purpose. The interior, glowing with multicoloured marble, mosaics and gilding, served as a museum in the Soviet era, but has now been returned to the church. It can hold a congregation of 10,000. A steep spiral staircase winds up to the colonnade around the dome, where you can enjoy superb views of the city while you catch your breath.

Next to the cathedral is a vast esplanade, bordered to the south by the Moyka. The wide Blue Bridge over it, leading to the Mariinsky Palace, was used until 1862 as a market place where landowners bought and sold their serfs.

Yusupov Palace

On the banks of the Moyka, at no. 94, a golden yellow façade and door topped by the coat of arms of the Yusupov princes denotes the palace of this grand family, on intimate terms with the tsars. One member of the family distinguished himself by assassinating Rasputin in 1916. The residence was rebuilt in 1830 and demonstrates the luxury typical of the period. The grand staircase, ceremonial rooms, ballroom, exquisite little theatre where Liszt played and Chaliapin sang, the oriental salon with its onyx fireplace and fountain form the happy blend of styles—neoclassicism, Renaissance, baroque, rococo—and rich materials —marble, gilding, silk, malachite—that came to be known as eclecticism (or historicism), appealing to all those who could afford such extravagance.

Mariinsky Theatre of Opera and Ballet

St Petersburg's most famous theatre stands in a quiet area south of St Isaac's. No matter what performance is being held, the theatre itself is a star attraction. The auditorium is a magnificent five-tiered gilded horseshoe, furnished in plush and crystal and topped off with flying angels. It dates from the 1870s but was badly damaged in World War II. Repairs began even before the siege was lifted and performances resumed in September

1944. Before the fall of communism, it was called the Kirov, after Stalin's deputy who was assassinated in 1934. Graduates of the world-famous Kirov ballet company who defected to the West included Nureyev, Makarova and Baryshnikov.

St Nicholas Cathedral

Close to the Mariinsky Theatre, beside the Kriukov Canal, this pastel blue church was designed by a pupil of Rastrelli. In the heart of the old sailors' district, it is one of the rare "Russified" churches of the town centre. Its façades, supported by sets of three columns decorated with throngs of cherubs, are topped by five golden domes.

Nevsky Prospekt

Cutting off a loop of the Neva, the city's main thoroughfare, drawn up under Peter the Great, runs for almost 5 km (3 miles) from the Admiralty in the west to the Alexander Nevsky Monastery in the east. From its beginnings, all the city's celebrities, its writers and musicians, took up residence close to the avenue. Its best-trodden section has always been that stretching from the Admiralty to the bridge over the Fontanka Canal, and on sunny days crowds of locals and tourists stroll up and down. The Champs-Elysées of St Petersburg is lined with department stores, hotels, cafés, restaurants, theatres and numerous churches. The 18th and 19th-century buildings on each side of the avenue are in a remarkable state of preservation, considering the impact of war, neglect, climate and sheer wear and tear. Historic associations abound.

West of the Avenue

Near the Admiralty end, just south of Palace Square, next to the Moyka bridge, is the Literary Café (no. 18) where Pushkin drank his last cup of chocolate before he was killed fighting a duel. A sign in Cyrillic letters discloses its original name: Café Wulf and Béranger.

Rastrelli's immense baroque Stroganov Palace (*Stroganovski Dvorets*) stands on the opposite side of the river. It's claimed that in the kitchens of this palace, a French chef concocted the original recipe for Bœuf Stroganov. The building is now used for temporary exhibitions of the Russian Museum.

Kazan Cathedral

The monumental Cathedral of Our Lady of Kazan, to give it its full name, forms a semicircular colonnaded embrace, recalling St Peter's in Rome. The impression is reinforced by the stone cupola on a drum-shaped tower. In front are the statues of Kutuzov and Barclay de Tolly, the generals who (along with "General Winter and General Snow") harried Napoleon's retreating army from Moscow back to Poland and beyond. The tomb of Kutuzov is just to the right of the entrance, surrounded by several French standards and the keys to the city, retrieved from the invaders.

Kazansky Sobor suffered the insult of being used during the Soviet era as a "Museum of the History of Religion and Atheism" (contrasting the supposed evils of the former and the rational good sense of the latter). Restoration is complete and church services are again being held.

Gostiny Dvor

The huge arcaded building (the name means merchants' yard) at no. 35 Nevsky Prospekt is St Petersburg's main department store, a galleried square with rows of individual shops selling local and Western goods. The most exclusive designer names are all together upstairs on the first floor.

The *Pasazh* arcade across the street at No. 48 is a similar shopping mall, a century old, with a good supermarket in the basement and all kinds of boutiques sheltered beneath its long glass roof.

Around Ostrovksi Square

This pleasant, airy little park, with numerous benches beneath the trees, is dominated by the imposing statue of Catherine II in majesty, surrounded by many of her intimate friends and relatives, and several of her lovers. On the west side of the square is the Russian National Library, where Lenin used to read at the end of the 19th century, as attested by a plaque. To the south, the large neoclassical building of the Alexandrinsky Theatre (formerly the Pushkin) is topped by a quadriga and decorated with a pretty frieze of masks. To the east is the garden of the Anichkov Palace.

Opposite the square, on the other side of Nevsky Prospekt, admire one of the town's most handsome Art Nouveau buildings, the Eliseev store (no. 56), which stands out with its big glass window. There's a gourmet grocery department on the ground floor—go inside if only to look at the stained glass, lamps and wooden counters in typical 1900s style.

Beloselsky-Belozersky Palace

For a time the city centre stopped at the Fontanka Canal which curves round into the Neva. Crossing over it is the Anichkov Bridge, embellished with four statues of rearing horses. On the 55 opposite bank you will notice the deep pink walls of the superb Beloselsky-Belozersky Palace, the former headquarters of the Communist Party and now a cultural centre. A row of muscular atlantes adorns the façade, and others hold up the grand staircase.

Dostoyevsky Museum

Make a short detour to this small museum between the Fontanka Canal and the Moscow station, set up in the last home of one of Russia's best-known writers. His life and work is documented by photographs, papers and personal belongings.

Alexander Nevsky Monastery

At the eastern end of Nevsky Prospekt, this great orthodox monastery was founded in 1712 by Peter the Great to house the relics of Prince Alexander "Nevsky", a Russian hero who defeated the Swedes at the battle of the Neva in 1240. The relics spent many years in the Hermitage before being repatriated here, where they are kept in a silver reliquary beneath a golden canopy. Services continued here during the Soviet era, attended mainly by a few old people; nowadays the church can be full to overflowing. There are two cemeteries next to the monastery; this is where Dostoyevsky, Tchaikovsky, Rimsky-Korsakov and many other famous Russians are buried.

From Arts Square to the Smolny Convent

The side street opposite Gostiny Dvor takes you past the opulent façade of the Europa Hotel to Ploshchad Iskusstv, a noble square centering on a park with a statue of Pushkin. Attributed to Rossi, the square is one of St Petersburg's finest architectural ensembles. As its focal point, the yellow and white Mikhailovsky Palace houses the State Russian Museum (*Russky Muzey*). It was built in 1825 for the Grand-Duke Michael, brother of Alexander I and Nicholas I. Beyond are the Summer Gardens and neighbouring palaces, and in the distance the Smolny Convent.

Russian Museum

St Petersburg's collection of Russian art is one of the largest in the world, only exceeded in quality by Moscow's Tretyakov Gallery. The magnificent icons begin with those from 12th-century Novgorod and include some by Andrey Rublyov. He was the first to impose a specific painting style for Russian icons, using rich colours, at the end of the 14th century. All the national schools of secular painters are here, from the 18th-century portraitists to the avant-garde of the 1920s. Look especially for the dramatic historical scenes by nationalists Nikolay Ge and Surikov; the Wanderers led by Repin, whose *Volga Boatmen* made him internationally famous; the rural scenes by Levitan; the visionary works of Vrubel; explosions of light by Bakst and Goncharova; and the revolutionary art of Kandinsky, Malevich, Rodchenko and Tatlin.

Church of the Resurrection

Behind the Russian Museum, you can cut back to the Neva following the Griboyedov Canal. Beside it stands a church built on the spot where Alexander II was assassinated in 1881 and also called the Church of the Spilled Blood *(Khram Spasa na Krovi).* It bears a striking resemblance to St Basil's in Moscow, with numerous colourful and gilded onion domes. Nothing was too fine for this shrine erected to the memory of the tsar: the interior walls, the supports, the domes are entirely covered with mosaics— 7000 sq m of them—while the inlaid floor and pink iconostasis were made from Italian marble. The canopy marks the precise place of the assassination and covers part of the old paved street that has been preserved in its original state.

Summer Gardens

Between two canals, close to the Neva, this is one of the city's most pleasant parks, with trees and statues lined up in formal precision, like those of the château of Versailles. It's an odd sight in winter when the statues are boxed up in wooden cases to protect them from the cold. This was one of the favourite parks of the 19th-century aristocracy.

In the northeastern corner of the park, the tiny Summer Palace *(Letny Dvorets),* in the vaguely Dutch style favoured by Peter the Great and sometimes called "Peter's baroque", was built soon after he founded the city. He is said to have helped to panel the interior walls himself.

Engineers' Castle

To the south, Ingenierni Zamok was built in monumental and defensive style for tsar Paul I (son of Catherine II), an acknowledged paranoiac. Fatefully, he was assassinated just 40 days after taking up residence in his castle. The building was used as an Engineering College and counted among its students a certain Dostoyevsky. It now houses galleries of imperial portraits.

Field of Mars

Across the peaceful Swan Canal, the Field of Mars was the principal parade ground of the elite

Lime trees shade the elegant paths of the Summer Gardens.

units of the tsar's army. The neoclassical Marble Palace nearby, built on the orders of Catherine II for Prince Gregory Orlov, one of her favourites, is used for temporary exhibitions organized by the Russian Museum.

Smolny Convent

One of Rastrelli's most enchanting confections stands next to a great bend in the Neva, 3 km (2 miles) to the east of the Summer Garden. A vision of turquoise and white, topped with a cluster of gilded onion domes, it was the cathedral church for the Smolny Convent and was built between 1746 57. It is now used for con-

certs and exhibitions. Four other churches were built within the same complex.

Smolny Institute

The October Revolution of 1917 was plotted behind the classical columns and yellow walls of the Institute, next to the church. Built in the early 19th century as as a boarding school for the daughters of the nobility, it was taken over by the Bolsheviks for their headquarters; Lenin lived and worked here for a time. Today it houses the offices of the mayor of St Petersburg, but the apartments of the former Soviet hero are open for visits.

The successive tsars all built summer residences in the St Petersburg region, each one more lavish than the last. Two of them are located near the Gulf of Finland, and two are inland.

Other historic cities can be visited from St Petersburg though they are much further away. Novgorod, 189 km (118 miles) to the southeast, and Pskov, 265 km (165 miles) to the southwest, have retained much of their past: masterpieces of medieval architecture and fine collections of icons.

Peterhof

About 32 km (20 miles) west of St Petersburg on the Gulf of Finland, Peterhof (or Petrodvorets) was the brainchild of Peter the Great. Begun in 1715 by Jean-Baptiste Leblond, it was originally intended to be a Russian Versailles, though on a smaller scale. The Empress Elizabeth gave Rastrelli the job of making it grander, adding wings, galleries and a chapel. World War II saw Peterhof badly damaged when the Germans occupied it, and completely gutted when they blew it up as they retreated in 1944. Restoration, relying on pre-war photos and drawings,

took several decades but is now completed. The chandeliers and paintings are originals—they were carried away into safekeeping during the hostilities and have now been returned to their rightful place.

The palace looks out onto the tumbling waters of the Grand Cascade, the largest of 150 fountains in the huge park which covers more than 1000 hectares (2,500 acres). Samson's Fountain at the top symbolizes Russia's victory over Sweden in 1709, with Samson forcing open the jaws of a lion to release a jet of water rising 20 m (65 ft) into the air. A fountain-lined canal leads to the Baltic shore, where a hovercraft brings visitors from St Petersburg. To the right of the main building (as you face the sea), Monplaisir is a cosy residence in the Dutch style favoured by Peter the Great. On the other side is Marly Palace, from where the tsar liked to contemplate his Baltic fleet.

Lomonosov

Former Oranienbaum, renamed in 1948 because it sounded too German, stands about 20 km (12 miles) west of Peterhof. The land was given by Peter the Great to

his minister, Prince Menshikov, but after Peter's death and Menshikov's banishment it became royal property. The effete Peter III, who only reigned for a few months, had a miniature palace, Peterstadt, built to go with the toy castle where he played with his (real) soldiers. After his murder, Catherine II turned the estate into a summer playground, complete with a switchback (*Katalnaya Gorka*), an early rollercoaster. Only its blue and white three-storey launching pavilion has survived.

The highlight is Catherine's sumptuous Chinese Palace designed by Rinaldi in rococo style; a second storey was added in the 1840s. The wooden parquet floors, inlaid panels on the walls and painted ceilings are the originals; unlike the other royal retreats, Lomonosov escaped the worst effects of World War II.

Tsarskoe Selo

Tsar's Village was renamed Pushkin, after the national poet who went to school here, but the original name has been revived. Like Peterhof, it served as a summer retreat for the imperial family. Tsarskoe Selo lies 28 km (17

From the palace at Peterhof the view reaches over the Grand Cascade to the Baltic.

miles) south of St Petersburg, and is easily reached by bus or train. The first Russian railway was in fact built so that the tsar and his suite could travel here easily. The domain was occupied by the Nazis for almost three years, from 1941 to 1944, and the palaces were looted and wrecked. The celebrated Amber Room, its walls lined with panels of amber, was dismantled and taken to Germany where it vanished in the chaos at the end of the war. After more than 20 years of painstaking restoration work, thanks to the financial contribution of the German government, it now looks like new and was reopened for the tricentenary of St Petersburg. Other rooms and the exterior were restored at the same time. The beautiful gardens and park are dotted with lakes, bathhouses and grottoes, statues and fountains.

Catherine Palace

One of Rastrelli's most elegant designs, with an ornate blue and white façade 300 m (1,000 ft) long, Catherine's Palace (*Yekaterininsky Dvorets*), the grandest at Tsarskoe Selo, was named after Peter the Great's widow, Catherine I. Later, Catherine II put her own stamp on it when she engaged a mysterious and virtually unknown Scot, Charles Cameron, to remodel many of the 61

rooms. Next to the palace he added a long classical gallery lined with Greek and Roman busts, depicting the ancient philosophers that Catherine so much admired. Beneath the golden domes, the interiors are resplendent with mirrors, gilding and chubby cherubs.

Alexander Palace

The much smaller Aleksandrovsky Dvorets has an almost homely look compared to its grand neighbour. The last tsar and his family lived here under house arrest in 1917–18 before being taken to Yekaterinburg, where they were eventually shot. The palace was built at the end of the 18th century for Alexander I, to a design by Quarenghi. It now contains a permanent exhibition devoted to its history and the life of the last members of the Romanov family.

Pavlovsk

Southeast of Tsarskoe Selo, the Pavlovsk estate was presented by Catherine the Great to her son, Paul, in 1777, to celebrate the birth of her first grandson, Alexander. Its palace was the masterpiece of her favourite architect, Cameron, although the eccentric Paul, who detested his mother and had to wait another 19 years before he came to the throne, had it remodelled by the Italians Quarenghi and Brenna. But the curved façade and several graceful pavilions spread around the 520 hectares of the estate are the pure inspiration of Cameron. The palace still carries memories of Maria Feodorovna, the wife of Paul I. She loved staying here more than anywhere else, and continued to beautify the rooms very tastefully after her husband was assassinated. Pavlosk was destroyed during World War II and was the first to be entirely restored.

Novgorod

Founded in 859 by the Varangian prince Rurik on the shores of the Volkhov, Novgorod-the-Great, a city of 240,000 inhabitants, shares with Kiev the honour of being the cradle of Russian culture. At the crossroads with the great trading routes between the Gulf of Finland and the Black Sea, on the route "from the Varangians to the Greeks", the town developed quickly.

In 1477 Ivan III of Moscow attacked and annexed it; until then it had been a feudal republic, independent of Kiev and governed by a citizens' assembly called the Vetche. It vanquished the Swedes in 1240 and under the

Restored to its former splendour, Catherine Palace at Tsarskoe Selo.

leadership of its prince Alexander Nevsky, defeated the Teutonic knights in 1242. Spared by the Tatar invasions, the merchant city played an exceptional role in the development of Russian arts and culture. During its Golden Age in the 14th century, Novgorod's wealthy merchants financed the construction of numerous churches. In style they were more simple than those of Kiev, with elegant, uncluttered lines, but the interiors were lavishly decorated with frescoes and splendid icons.

In the 15th century the city began to decline: with the construction of St Petersburg it dwindled into little more than a provincial town. It was severely damaged during World War II but has been restored since then, and has preserved a unique cultural heritage.

The Kremlin

On the left bank of the Volkhov, the oval-shaped 9-towered kremlin was built between the 11th and 15th centuries. Inside are several churches, the cathedral of St Sophia, a museum, a concert hall and various other monuments. You can join a group tour or wander around on your own.

Cathedral of St Sophia

The imposing five-domed Byzantine cathedral was built between 1045 and 1050), and is one of the oldest churches in Russia. It is exceptionally tall, at 40 m (131 ft). The west doors, made in Magdeburg but brought here from the Swedish town of Sigtuna, are decorated with biblical scenes in bronze relief. In the lower left corner are portraits of the two craftsmen who cast the bronze; the central figure is the Russian Avraam, who assembled the doors. Inside are icons dating back to the 14th century, and 19th-century frescoes.

Chamber of Facets

Behind the cathedral, this was part of a 15th-century reception hall, now containing a collection of icons and various treasures gathered from churches around the region.

Millennium of Russia Monument

The round bronze monument in the middle of the kremlin was inaugurated in 1862 to commemorate Rurik's arrival in Novgorod 1000 years previously. At the top is the Motherland, and among the more than 100 figures encircling the lower slopes are Rurik, Peter the Great, Catherine the Great, Alexander Nevsky, the poet Pushkin, composer Glinka and many other literary and artistic figures, military heroes and statesmen.

Museum of History and Art

The large building behind the Millennium Monument displays a large collection of early icons, exceptional miniatures and rare birch bark manuscripts.

Yaroslav's Court

On the right bank, in the heart of the old market district, the palace of the Novgorod princes was the medieval equivalent of a mall, with no less than 1500 boutiques in the 16th century. Today it is an airy, gardened square, bordered to the north by the market arcades (with a superb view of the kremlin). Among the seven churches to the east, the Court Cathedral of St Nicholas (1113), has preserved fragments of ancient frescoes, while the 14th-century Church of our Saviour-at-Illino boasts the only surviving frescoes of the Byzantine artist Theophanes the Greek.

Surroundings

On the left bank of the river, near Ilmen lake, 3 km (2 miles) out of town, is the 12th-century Monastery of St George; the princes of Novgorod are buried in its cathedral.

A short walk away, hidden away in the forest, the Vitoslavlitsy Museum of Wooden Architecture displays a collection of wooden churches and peasant houses.

Pskov

Mentioned in chronicles as far back as 903, this city broke away from Novgorod in 1348 and developed rapidly thanks to commerce. It suffered severe damage in 1941 but still retains many architectural treasures.

Kremlin

Built on a spur at the confluence of the Pskova and Velikaya rivers, it encloses Trinity Cathedral whose gilded domes can be seen from 30 km (18 miles) away.

History and Art Museum

Three rooms in the palace of a wealthy 17th-century merchant, Sergei Pogankin, display icons of the Pskov school, where red and green dominate (14th–15th centuries). There is also a collection of Russian silver and applied arts.

Mirozhsky Monastery

This 12th-century monastery is particularly noted for the Cathedral of the Transfiguration of the Saviour (1136). Its superb 12th-century frescoes were restored by Dimitri Briagine in 1969.

Pechory Monastery

North of the city, this fabulous working fortified monastery was founded in 1473 in a ravine full of hermits' caves. You can visit the catacombs and several 16th and 18th- century churches.

➡ LAKE AND RIVER CRUISES

The Neva and Volga from St Petersburg to Astrakhan,
The Volga-Don Canal from Volgograd to Rostov-on-Don,
The Oka from Nizhny Novgorod to Moscow,
The Kama from Kazan to Perm

A journey on her great lakes and rivers reveals a different face of Russia, more ancient, more primitive, an image that could be drawn from old picture books. The sombre forests of the north fringe the edges of lakes so wide that you lose sight of the shore. The river banks are dotted with picturesque little wooden houses and churches topped with clustered onion domes.

Comfortable river cruisers ply between St Petersburg and Moscow, others from Moscow down to Astrakhan, almost to the delta of the Volga on the Caspian Sea. For variety, some make detours along the tributaries of the Volga—the Oka and the Kama. Whatever itinerary you choose, you will see the heart of the country and get a grasp of its immensity. On board, the degree of luxury varies—and with it the price of the cruise. Russian, German or American operators manage the accommodation and restaurants; it is also possible to select a cruise where only English (or German) is used for announcements and on guided tours. Of course, all cruises go in both directions, up and downriver.

The Neva and Volga from St Petersburg to Astrakhan

From Peter the Great's "Window on the West", ships take 10 to 14 days to reach Moscow by way of the Neva, Svir and Volga rivers and the canals connecting them. From the junction at Lake Rybinsk, some cruises make directly for Moscow, others head down the Volga to Yaroslavl and Kostroma before turning back to Rybinsk and the capital—or continuing downriver to Kazan, Volgograd and Astrakhan.

The Neva

It meanders for a mere 74 km (46 miles) from Lake Ladoga to the Gulf of Finland, but the Neva river is of vast significance to Russian history. It was the reason Peter the Great selected the site for his new capital; it defines the shape of the city and creates its unforgettable vistas, although its floods have often inundated the lower-lying areas. It brings damp, fog and winter ice, but also the magical "white nights" in midsummer. Because of its exceptional depth—8 to 24 m (26–78 ft)—even large ships can sail into the centre of the city when the bridges are opened. It's worth staying up late to see this spectacular aspect of the river.

Lake Ladoga

Europe's largest lake, with an area of 18,000 sq km (7,000 sq miles) stretches far to the north, into the pine forests of Karelia. Its shores now lie entirely within Russia—the Finns were pushed away at the end of World War II. Rich in stocks of salmon and sturgeon, the lake freezes over from November to April. During the winters of the 990-day Siege of Leningrad, trucks driving across the ice provided the only lifeline into the city.

Petrokrepost

The fortress (Schlüsselburg) guarding the passage of the Neva where it leaves Lake Ladoga was built by the city-state of Novgorod when it ruled this area in the 14th century. The Swedes took it in 1611, but Peter the Great recovered it in 1702. It served as a prison—Lenin's brother was held here—and was turned into a Museum of the Revolution in 1920.

Valaam

Of some 500 islands in the lake, Valaam is notable for the Monastery of the Transfiguration, formerly one of the most important centres of the Orthodox Church. In the 14th century, it is said to have numbered 200 churches and hermitages, but fighting between Novgorod and Sweden led to its decline. Peter the Great restored it; in the 19th century the tranquil atmosphere attracted artists and writers.

After 1917, it became part of Finland but fell to Soviet forces during the Winter War of 1940. The monks had already fled, carrying many of their icons and precious manuscripts with them; the monastery was closed and left to decay. In 1992, it was at last returned to the Church, and limited restoration began.

The Svir

From the southern end of Lake Ladoga, cruise boats enter the Svir river (labelled the "Blue Route") and head upstream against a gentle current, stopping here and there at a village such as Svirstroy for a barbecue or picnic ashore. The hinterland is a vast nature reserve, the haunt of elk, bear and lynx, with seals sporting in the water. After 215 km (134 miles), the Svir opens into a lake almost as large as Ladoga.

Lake Onega

With 1,300 islands, pure water, hidden coves and beaches, abundant wildlife and virgin forest within reach, Onega became a 67 holiday retreat for a privileged few under the Soviet regime. Now more people come to relax, sail in summer or go cross-country skiing in springtime. The lake's northern tip is linked to the Arctic by the White Sea Canal, built by forced labour during Stalin's time.

Petrozavodsk

On the western shore of Lake Onega, the capital of the Karelia region was founded by Peter the Great to build ships and make guns for his war with Sweden; its name means "Peter's factory town". There's an Art Museum with icons from the island of Kizhi, a cathedral, university, hotels and shops. Souvenirs include attractive Karelian embroidery and national costume. But the principal reason visitors come to Petrozavodsk is to take a trip on their own cruise boat or by hydrofoil to Kizhi, an enchanting island 70 km (43 miles) away.

The wooden domes of Kizhi's Church of the Transfiguration glint like silver.

Kizhi Island

In the northern part of Lake Onega, the last Ice Age left a strange landscape of long, ribbon-like peninsulas and islands. The largest, Kizhi (1 km wide and 6 km long) has the finest assembly of ancient wooden churches in Russia, including the fairy-tale 22-domed Church of the Transfiguration, built in 1714. The silvery overlapping tiles of the bulbs are made from aspen wood. Within the same wooden-walled compound are an octagonal bell tower of 1862 and the little nine-domed Church of the Intercession, built in 1764 without the use of a single nail.

A short walk south, the oldest building here is the 13th-century Church of the Resurrection of Lazarus, said to cure toothache. South again towards the end of the promontory are the 18th-century Chapel of the Archangel Michael, wooden mills, houses and farm buildings collected from all over Karelia to form an open-air folk museum of architecture and daily life.

Volga-Baltic Canal

In 1810, Lake Onega and the Kovya river were linked by canal; goods had previously to be hauled over land between the two. The little town of Vytegra enjoyed a period of prosperity, ended by the coming of the railway later in the 19th century. Then, in 1964, the Volga-Baltic Canal was completed, able to take ships of up to 5,000 tonnes. Linking rivers and lakes, it runs for 360 km (223 miles) from Lake Onega to the upper Volga river. Locks carry it to a height of 113 m (370 ft), down again to the Kovya river and on through forests and picturesque countryside until it opens into the broad expanse of the White Lake.

Goritsy

South of the White Lake, Goritsy is the starting point for an excursion to the 15th-century Kirillo-Belozersky Monastery, 15 km (9 miles) away. St Cyril was 60 years old when he left Moscow to live the life of a hermit on the shores of the White Lake. Pilgrims soon followed his example and the site developed into an influential monastery, supported by the tsars. At the height of its power, the monastery owned 400 villages and 20,000 serfs. In the 20th century it was turned into a museum. Within its fortress-like walls (which can be toured) you can visit the wooden chapel built by St Cyril, the monastery buildings and the village which grew up around them. Do not miss the museum where 200 splendid icons dating from the 15th to 17th centuries are displayed alongside fine pieces of lace and birchbark sandals.

The Sheksna

The dilapidated Resurrection Monastery beside the Sheksna river near Goritsy dates from the 16th century. It is currently being restored under the direction of two courageous nuns. There is a holy atmosphere, despite certain unfortunate incidents in the past: the fourth wife of Ivan the Terrible (he had seven altogether) was incarcerated behind its walls, and upon his orders the founder of the convent, Princess Efrossinia of Moscow, was drowned in the Sheksna.

Cruise boats usually make a stop at Irma on the banks of the Sheksna for a lunch of shashlik and a chance to meet some of the villagers.

At the town of Sheksna, two locks lower the level of the waterway by 13 m (42 ft) and a dam provides hydroelectric power for the region.

Lake Rybinsk

At Cherepovets a suspension bridge over a kilometre long straddles the Sheksna, 85 m (279 ft) above the river. The Sheksna flows into the huge reservoir of Lake Rybinsk which formed by the damming of the Volga, one of Stalin's projects in 1932. When the dam was filled in 1941, 700

villages were drowned; this was during the Stalin era and, needless to say, the population was not consulted on the matter, nor on their relocation. More than 600 rivers pour into the reservoir, which is about 5 m (16 ft) deep. Boats leaving it have to go through several locks, descending 16 m (52 ft).

The reservoir is named after the town of Rybinsk, which had been in existence as a fishing centre since the 12th century—its name derives from *ryba*, fish. It became a great commercial port after construction of the Marie Canal. From 1984 to 1989 it was called Andropov, in honour of the former KGB boss who was briefly Soviet president.

The Volga

Cruising along the Volga brings you close to the country's Slavic soul. The river has always been known affectionately to Russians as *matushka*, "little mother", and sentimental folk songs refer to it that way. The first part of the cruise passes through lush and wooded countryside, before penetrating deeper into the steppe and semi-desert savannah. In the middle reaches of the river, the contrast between the western bank's mountainous scenery and the eastern bank's flatness is striking. The diversity of the peoples along the river banks is as marked as the variety of the landscapes. If the principal ethnic group is Russian, along the middle and lower reaches of the Volga there are Tatars, Chuvashians, Marii and Kalmucks, not forgetting descendants of the Germans who settled here in the 18th century during the reign of Catherine the Great, herself of German origin.

In the 18th century, plans were made to link the Volga by canals to five seas: the Baltic, the Arctic White Sea, the Sea of Azov, the Black Sea and the Caspian. This was finally realised in the 1950s, with Moscow also joined to the system by the Moskva-Volga Canal. In summer, these busy waterways carry pleasure craft, cruisers with up to 300 passengers and a fascinating variety of cargo vessels. From November to April, the rivers and canals of central and northern Russia are frozen over.

Mychkino

Some cruise ships make a stop at this picturesque little town founded in 1238, near the mouth of the Yukhot, downriver from Uglich. Called Little St Petersburg because of the classic design of its architecture, it has the world's only Mouse Museum. According to legend, a local prince was saved from a snakebite by a little mouse that pre-

---

THE VOLGA

From its source on the Valdai Plateau northwest of Moscow, the Volga spreads out at Astrakhan after 3,700 km (2,300 miles). It forms a delta 150 km (93 miles) wide before emptying into the Caspian Sea. The four great Siberian rivers—the Lena, the Amur, the Yenisey and the Ob—are longer than the Volga, but it is still the longest river in Europe.

---

vented him from falling unconscious by trotting all over his face. In gratitude, the prince built a chapel on the spot where the mouse saved his life, and later, the village that grew up around it was called Mychkino from *mychka*, Russian for mouse.

Uglich

Arriving by boat in Uglich, upstream from Rybinsk, is as romantic an introduction to the city (40,000 inhabitants) as you could wish for. Excursions are generally arranged to visit the kremlin, close to the landing stage. The small industrial town founded in 1148, known today for its Chaika watch factory, was the scene of a terrible tragedy. Ivan the Terrible bequeathed it to his infant son Dmitry, in effect banishing him there with his mother Maria Nagaïa (the tsar's seventh and last wife) and relatives, while his slow-witted brother Fyodor became tsar and Boris Godunov regent. In 1591, Dmitry, then aged nine, was murdered. He was declared a saint in 1606, and the Church of St Dmitry on the Blood, red and white with five blue star-spangled domes, was built in 1692 where his body was found, within the kremlin beside the river. The church contains an exhibition of icons of the Moscow, Uglich and Kostroma schools, a handsome cast-iron floor, and a bell, brought back from its exile in Tobolsk, where it was sent as punishment for tolling the death of the tsarevitch.

Nearby is the Cathedral of the Transfiguration, with a high vaulted ceiling. It was rebuilt in the Narychkine, or Russian baroque style in 1713. Inside is an impressive seven-tiered icon screen and beautiful frescoes. If you are lucky you may be here at the time when a quatuor gives an *a cappella* hymn recital. Outside, the gilded bell tower, 37 m (121 ft) high, houses an antique shop.

The oldest building in the town is the 15th-century Dmitry's Palace, now a museum documenting his life.

Outside the walls of the kremlin is the 17th-century Resurrection Monastery, in poor condition, together with the church of St John the Baptist and the elegant St Alexis monastery, dating from 1371.

Kaliazin

Some 50 km (30 miles) after Uglich, a plaintive sight greets your eyes; the church tower of Kaliazin showing above the water while the rest of the town with its 15th-century convent lies submerged. It was covered after the construction of the Uglich barrage, downstream.

Tver

On the upper Volga, 140 km (90 miles) northwest of Moscow, Tver was first mentioned in 1135 and was Moscow's principal rival throughout the 14th and 15th centuries. In 1763, almost all its historic buildings were destroyed in a fire. They were replaced by others in the baroque and neoclassical styles on the orders of Catherine the Great—Tver was an important staging post on the way to St Petersburg. Her palace is now the regional museum and art gallery. The Church of the White Trinity (*Belaya Troitsa*) is a rare (and the oldest) pre-fire survivor, from 1563. A statue honours the local merchant Nikitin who sailed to India 30 years before Vasco da Gama. From 1931 to 1991, Tver was rebaptised Kalinin, after one of Stalin's companions.

Moskva-Volga Canal

Peter the Great dreamed of linking Moscow to the Volga, but the first canal was not completed till 1825, to ferry the building materials of Moscow's Cathedral of Christ the Saviour. With the coming of the railways, the importance of the canal declined greatly, but in 1937 it was reopened after renovation work carried over five years out by prisoners from the gulag. From the Ivankovo reservoir, the 128-km (80-mile) canal reaches the capital in about ten hours by way of six locks—hence its nickname, the Light Blue Staircase.

Tutayev

To reach Yaroslavl (see p. 41) and Kostroma (p. 42), boats go down the Volga, cross the Rybinsk Reservoir from west to east, then, like the river, change direction and head south. Tutayev, named in honour of one of the heroes of the Red Army, used to be called Romanov. It flourished at the end of the 18th century when it was famous for painted icons, boat-building, weaving and goldsmiths. Many of its churches date from that era and some are visible from the river. the wooden houses and the "old Russia" atmosphere attract many artists.

Tolga Monastery, 700 years old, stands on the river bank in the middle of a forest. It was closed in 1926 and returned to the Orthodox Church in 1988; nuns are again in residence.

THE SIX STEPS

Six locks are required to allow the boats that take the Moscow Canal to reach the Volga or the capital. They all have identical dimensions, 290 by 30 by 5.5 m (951 by 98 by 18 ft) but each one has its peculiarities. To get to Moscow, you will stop at km 165 and Lock No. 1, where the Volga joins the Moscow Canal. As the ship rises by 11 m (36 ft), notice the unusual cylindrical gates. At km 151 and Lock No. 2, surrounded by flower beds, the figures on the towers represent Russian customs officials. Lock No. 3, near the town of Yachroma, raises the ships by 8 m (26 ft), as does No. 4. The last three locks are quite close together. At km 96, Lock No. 5 has a rather heavy architectural style: in front of the upriver towers is the figure of a mysterious young woman carrying a sailing ship, while the downriver towers are topped by colonnaded viewing platforms. You rise another 8 m (26 ft here), as at Lock No. 6 at km 93. At this last lock, sculpted figures represent the workers and gulag prisoners who built the canal.

Approaching Yaroslavl, the oldest city on the Volga, the river spreads, serene and majestic, to a width of 800 m (2,625 ft).

Plios

This pretty village lies some 40 km (25 miles) downstream from Kostroma. Russian painters such as Ilya Repin (1844–1930) and Isaak Levitan (1860–1900) enjoyed staying here at the end of the 19th century. In Levitan's house, now a museum, you can see from his landscapes how little the rural scene has changed.

Gorodets

In 1152, Prince Yuri Dolgoruki founded Gorodets on the left bank of the Volga, to protect the principality of Suzdal from Bulgar invasion. Today it is a picturesque little town of 35,000, 70 km (43 miles) northwest of Nizhny Novgorod. It was here, in the Fedorovsky monastery, that Alexander Nevsky died in 1263. In the 18th century Gorodets was a market village. Naval construction flourished in the 19th century. The town is still renowned for its woodcarvings and gingerbread moulds, a tradition that dates back to the 17th century.

Intricate window decoration on the Church of the Nativity in Nizhny Novgorod.

Khokhloma

Cruise ships often organize excursions to this charming village, where the traditional red and gold wood bowls and platters are made. The narrow streets are lined with neat little wooden *isbas*, each one more elegant than its neighbour, with finely carved window frames. The Regional Museum displays intricate woodcarvings, window cornices, doorposts, everyday objects from peasant homes, spinning wheels, looms, and so on.

Nizhny Novgorod

At the confluence of the Oka and the Volga, Nizhny Novgorod is the third-largest town of Russia (2 million inhabitants), surpassed only by Moscow and St Petersburg. The city was founded in 1221. After the Mongols were driven out of Russia at the end of the 15th century, Nizhny Novgorod actively engaged in trade with Moscow via the Moskva and the Volga, and enjoyed a period of great prosperity, especially since 1817 when trade fairs were first held here. Streets, churches, inns and spas sprang up everywhere. The city was renamed Gorky in 1932, and it continued to grow after World War II, becoming a centre for industry and armaments, and consequently off-limits for foreigners. It achieved dubious fame from 75

1980 to 1986 as the place of exile of the physicist Andrei Sakharov, winner of the Nobel Peace Prize. This is now all in the past. In 1991 the town returned to its oiginal name and in 1995 the fair or *yarmarka*, (from the German for "annual market") celebrated its centennial. It has once again become a yearly event. The imposing kremlin in the upper city was first erected as a fort in the second half of the 14th century and rebuilt in the early 16th century). Among the other sights in the city are the Central Bank of Russia (1913) with handsome interior decoration inspired by Russian folklore; the Alexander Nevsky Cathedral; the 18th-century Church of the Nativity (Stroganov), with superb sculptures in white stone; and Bolchaya Pokrovskaya, a pedestrian street. The principal museums are devoted to Maxim Gorky: in the house where the writer lived from 1868 to 1884, and the romantic Kachirin house, where he spent his childhood with his grandparents. You can also visit Sakharov's apartment, where the scientist and his wife Elena Bonner spent their years of exile. Nizhny Novgorod is also the

Suyumbik tower, leaning slightly in the kremlin of Kazan.

home of the Volga car factory. If you have visited Moscow, you will have seen the yellow taxis and long black limousines of the party officials—all Volgas from the GAZ works here.

Kozmodemiansk

Shortly after Nizhny Novgorod, the Volga passes through the Republic of the Marii, Mari El, whose capital is Yoshkar-Ola. By the time you reach Kozmodemiansk, a typical provincial city, the river has widened to almost 2 km (a mile). The economy of this town of merchants and traders was based on timber. Its charm lies in the handsome private mansions that belonged to wealthy merchants. They are trimmed with intricate woodcarvings.

Cheboksary

Capital of the Chuvash Republic, with 420,000 inhabitants, this ancient town (founded in 1469) is located on the right bank of the Volga. The Muslim Chuvashians were forced to convert to Orthodox Christianity in the 16th century. The Trinity Monastery, which was founded in the 16th century under Ivan the Terrible, was transformed into a cultural centre after the Revolution, then served as a theatre and a hotel. It now belongs once more to the Orthodox Church. The industrialization of the entire Volga

basin under the Soviets had dramatic consequences for Cheboksary (and many other cities on the river) when the historic centre of the town was flooded as a result of the construction of a hydroelectric plant in the 1970s. At the same time, the building of a whole system of locks, dams and power stations was responsible for the disappearance of 2500 villages and thousands of historic monuments.

Apart from the Trinity Monastery, you can visit the 17th-century Church of the Presentation, that of the Dormition (1763) and of the Resurrection (1702), as well as an art gallery showing works of 19th and 20th-century Russian artists. This is also the birthplace of the great Bolshoy ballet dancer Anna Pavlova.

Sviask

Alone in the middle of the river, the little island of Sviask has only one church, one monastery and a handful of houses.

Kazan

The Volga now flows through the Tatar Autonomous Republic (Tatarstan), a sovereign state since 1992. Its picturesque capital, 700 km (434 miles) east of Moscow on the left bank of the Volga, is a town of 1 million inhabitants, of whom 55 per cent are of Russian origin and 45 per cent Tatar. Settled in Kazan, the Tatars were for a long time a threat to the power of the tsars. During the rule of Ivan the Terrible, in 1552, the Russians invaded, extending their frontiers to the east. St Basil's Cathedral in Moscow's Red Square was built to commemorate this victory. In 1774, Pugachev and his Cossacks destroyed Kazan; it was rebuilt under Catherine II. In the 20th century it was, like Nizhny Novgorod, cut off from the rest of the world for political reasons.

Modelled on the one in Moscow, the kremlin built by Ivan the Terrible on the ruins of a mosque is the symbol of Russian power. You should also see the Cathedral of Saints Peter and Paul, built on the orders of Peter the Great, and the 18th-century Marchani Mosque. The Cathedral of the Annunciation, built in 1562, does not resemble in the least St Basil's Cathedral, even though it was designed by the same architect, Postnik. Near the Suyumbik leaning tower is the huge modern mosque of Koul Cherif with turquoise minarets, financed by Saudi Arabia and still undergoing construction.

Kazan is the birthplace of the Russian opera singer Chaliapin, and of the great ballet dancer Rudolf Nureyev. A dance festival is held in summer. Maxim Gorky also lived and worked here. An important university town, Kazan counted among its students Lenin, who began to study law here in 1887 (he was soon sent down for his subversive ideas).

To soak up some of Kazan's oriental atmosphere, stroll along Bauman Street, and explore the colourful markets. Traditions are still upheld and illustrated by lively festivals such as Sabantui, held in June. Kazan is in the throes of preparation for the celebration of its ten centuries of existence, in 2005.

Raifa Monastery

In an enchanting setting some 20 km (12 miles) west of Kazan, the 17th-century monastery houses a famous icon of the Virgin of Georgia. At one time it had 17 churches. The monastery was closed in 1928 and used as a detention centre for young offenders. It re-opened for worship in 1990 and since then has been restored. A hotel was built beside a lake for the numerous pilgrims that flock here.

Kuybyshev Lake

Below Kazan, the Volga makes a sharp turn to the south and enters the artificial Kuybyshev Lake, at the confluence with the Kama. This stretch of the river was sparsely inhabited but after the October Revolution was heavily industrialized and now plays an important role in the country's economy. It dates from the construction, in 1955–57, of the Volga hydroelectric power plant in the town of Togliatti. This is one of the largest stretches of water in Russia, covering 6,450 sq km (2,580 sq miles). The waters brought by the Kama double the flow of the Volga.

Simbirsk (Ulyanovsk)

Founded in 1648 on the banks of Kuybyshev Lake as a fortified outpost of the Russian Empire, Simbirsk traded actively with Asia. Today, the town of 45,000 inhabitants is mostly known for its connections with Vladimir Ilyich Ulyanov, otherwise known as Lenin, who was born and lived here up to the age of 23. From 1970, the historic centre was transformed into a vast monument to his memory. The house in which he was born, now a museum, is surrounded by delightful 19th-century wooden houses, with every mod. con., where the town's worthies live. Thirty of its original 36 churches were destroyed; some have been rebuilt and today there are 10 in activity, such as All Saints, resurrected in 1998. A Cathedral of the Ascension is planned for the edge of town, and in the centre, the Church of the Trinity will be re-erected on its original site.

While you are here you can also look around the Goncharov Museum in the house where the writer was born. He gained fame for his novel *Oblomov*.

Togliatti

This industrial town stretching around a huge loop of the Volga was built at the end of the 1960s after the construction of the Kuybyshev hydroelectric plant, at the same time as the enormous VAZ factory where Lada cars are manufactured.

Samara

Known in the Soviet era as Kuybyshev, Samara was also founded in the 16th century as an outpost of the empire. Under the communist regime it became a centre for the armament and space industries. At the time, cruise ships carrying foreign passengers were only allowed to sail through the town in the middle of the night. The town is also home of the Rossia choolate factory and the Rodnik vodka distillery. Among the other curiosities, you might like to visit the State Museum of Astronautics in the Aviation University. The Municipal Theatre, a fine building of red brick with delicate white decoration, bears the name of Maxim Gorky, who lived and worked here for several years. A Museum of Literature was set up 79

Soldiers guard the eternal flame in Volgograd's Hall of Valour.

in his house. You can also see Stalin's bunker. The splendid Fine Arts Museum, in a 19th-century private mansion, has a good collection of Russian paintings from the 16th to 20th centuries (Repin, Levitan, Surikov, Malevich, Shishkin and others).

Saratov

The town was founded in 1590 on the upper side of the river, and spread across the Volga to the opposite bank in 1674. The bridge built across the river in 1965 is one of the longest in Europe. This city of 900,000 inhabitants is very lively and the atmosphere cheerful, but many of its monuments are in dire need of restoration. The 17th-century Trinity Cathedral, in Narychkin baroque style, stands in the centre of town. Walking towards Chernichevski Square, you will cross "Lime Tree Park", where one avenue was reserved for girls, the other for boys. On the right-hand side stands Utoli Moya Pechali Church (1907), topped by a cluster of small onion domes, and opposite, pedestrian Kirov Street, lined with elms. In the Radichev Museum of Art you can admire the works of many avant-garde painters which were fortunately hidden away in the provinces before Stalin could get his hands on them. Both Gorky and Chaliapin lived in this town and had jobs working at the port.

The Saratov Reservoir was filled in 1967–68. Its area is 1,831 sq km (732 sq miles), with an average depth of 8 m (26 ft), but plumbing to 30 m (98 ft in places.

Sea of Volgograd

Soon after Saratov, at the Balakovo Dam, the ships enter a huge reservoir known as the Sea of Volgograd. When the dam was built, the level of the Volga increased by 27 m (88 ft). The reservoir stretches downriver for 627 km (389 miles), covering an area of 3,470 sq km (1,388 sq miles). Whether you look to port or to starboard, the landscape is a flat expanse of agricultural land, then steppe and semi-desert all the way down to Volgograd.

Volgograd

First called Tsaritsyn, the town was renamed Stalingrad in 1925 then Volgograd, "town on the Volga", in 1961. Its original name is gradually reappearing on maps. Tsaritsyn started life as a fortified frontier town; it was drawn into the uprisings of the Cossacks and peasants led by Razin and Pugachev, and played an important part in the civil war of 1917–18. It acquired a sinister notoriety during World War II at the time of the Battle of Stalingrad, which cost the lives of more than 150,000 German and Russian troops.

It is difficult to miss the gigantic statue of the Motherland Monument, standing 70 m (230 ft) tall —85 m (280 ft) to the tip of her sword—on Mamayev hill, bitterly contested during the fighting of 1942–43. Bearing witness to the horrors of war, photographs of the battle are displayed in the panoramic museum of the "Hall of Valour". The names of 7200 soldiers who fell in combat are inscribed on the walls, while Schumann's *Traümerei* (Dreaming) plays over and over again. Soldiers stand as guard of honour in front of the eternal flame held in a huge raised hand.

Other witnesses of the past in Volgograd are the ruins of a flour mill, the Pavlov house, an open-air exhibition of ancient weapons and a poplar tree that survived hostilities and has become a protected monument.

Downriver from Volgograd, the river turns suddenly to the southeast and crosses the steppe towards Astrakhan.

Nikolskoye

Halfway between Volgograd and Astrakhan, cruise boats often make a stop here for a picnic or barbecue on a wide sandy beach. You can even go for a swim!

Astrakhan

This town of 500,000 inhabitants was founded by the Tatars in the 13th century on the left bank of the Volga. Beyond it, the river splits up into 800 arms that flow into the Caspian Sea some 100 km (60 miles) away. Apart from Russians, who account for more than 70 per cent of the population, Tatars, Kalmucks, Kirghiz and Kazaks live in this town. After its conquest by Ivan the Terrible in 1558, Astrakhan was rebuilt on the same bank. Today it spreads over 11 islands linked together by bridges, a cluster of districts of low-lying houses. The main source of income is fish. Wander around, drinking in the typical atmosphere, and climb up to the sumptuous 16th-century kremlin, high on a hilltop. Inside its walls, the Assumption Cathedral was built in 1698 by a serf, Dorofey Myakitchev. The neighbouring Trinity Cathedral is more modest. A huge and colourful market specializes in dried fish, and you may see poachers discreetly trying to sell caviar.

If you have time, visit the Kustodiev Museum of Fine Arts and the appealing Museum of Local History and Architecture.

Volga Delta

Astrakhan is a base for excursions to the Volga Delta, where the waters shelter pike, belugas and sturgeon—90 per cent of the world's sturgeon population lives in the Caspian Sea.

The delta is now a Biosphere Reserve under the protection of UNESCO. It abounds in exceptional flora and fauna.

The Volga-Don Canal

The Volga and the Don have been linked since 1952 by the Volga-Don canal, 101 km (62 miles) long. Some boats leaving Volgograd head southwest, through the historic lands of the Don Cossacks, world-famous for their choirs. They also practise traditional equestrian skills and folk dancing, and not only for the tourists.

Rostov-on-Don

The town itself, founded in the 18th century and home to about a million people, has little to see other than the central market, two parks and a museum of local history, but there are some interesting excursions to visit the old and new capitals of the Don Cossacks.

On the banks of the Don, some 30 km (18 miles) from Rostov, is the town of Starocherkask, the Don Cossacks' capital for 200 years. In 1805 it was replaced by Novocherkask, 40 km (25 miles) northeast of Rostov. This is the peaceful setting of the novel *And Quiet Flows the Don* by Mikhail

Fish, salted and dried, sold with a smile in the market of Astrakhan.

Sholokov, who received the Nobel Prize for Literature in 1965. The book describes the life of the Don Cossacks before and after World War I and during the civil war.

The Oka from Nizhny Novgorod to Moscow

The Oka, a tributary on the right bank of the Volga, flows for 1,480 km (919 miles) through densely populated agricultural and industrial areas before entering it at Nizhny Novgorod, bringing 1,200 cu m of water per second. Its hydrographic basin covers 245,000 sq km (98,000 sq miles) in western Russia.

Pavlovo

On the right bank of the Oka, 78 km (48 miles) southwest of Nizhny Novgorod, this small town of 72,000 inhabitants was a staging post on the route to and from Moscow in the 16th century. It later became known as a centre of cutlery manufacture and metalworking. By the 19th century it had developed into an important centre of the metallurgical industry and mechanical construction; today it produces the well-known PAZ buses, garden tools, cutlery and various metal souvenirs.

There are several imposing public buildings dating from the

18th and 19th centuries, and a regional museum displaying an impressive collection of metal objects created by the best local craftsmen. Pavlovo is also known for its traditional goose fights held every year since the 16th century, as well as its canary singing competitions!

Murom

Next stop is Murom (130,000 inhabitants) on the left bank of the Oka. Mentioned in chronicles since 862, the city became part of the Principality of Ryazan-Murom in 1097. It was invaded by Bulgarians and Tatars, and annexed by Moscow at the beginning of the 15th century. Its economy was based on commerce, and from the 19th century onwards, its industry developed, specializing in mechanical construction and textiles.

The old town has preserved numerous monasteries and churches of the 16th to 17th centuries. To the south, the monumental five-domed Transfiguration Cathedral in St Saviour's Monastery (11th century) was rebuilt in the second half of the 16th century. Nearby is the humble little church of Cosme and Damian (1565). The architect is said to be Postnik, who designed St Basil's Cathedral on Moscow's Red Square. Two other religious complexes stand out:

Trinity Monastery with its cathedral (1642–43) decorated with porcelain tiles, enclosed with its belltower (1652) by an early-19th century wall; and close by, the Annunciation Monastery and its 16th–17th-century cathedral. Inside this is a baroque icon screen covered in 12th and 13th-century icons. A little further away stands the Church of the Resurrection (1659), and almost at the water's edge St Nicholas Church (1700–17). As you stroll around town you will notice the modern railway station and Empire-style houses.

From Murom, a bus trip takes you to two gems on the Golden Ring: Vladimir (see p. 39) and Suzdal (p. 40), located respectively 137 and 175 km (85 and 108 miles) to the southwest.

Kasimov

This ancient city, founded in 1152 by prince Yuri Dolgoruki, was called at the time Gorodets Mecherskiy. It owes its present name to Kassim, the Khan of Kazan. He was granted the city as a privilege in 1471 by the Grand-Prince of Moscow, Vassili II, in gratitude for having joined the Russian armies in 1446. Numerous Tatars followed the Khan to Kasimov. Some interesting Tatar monuments date from that period: a white stone mosque rebuilt in the 18th century on the site of the 15th-century original and its minaret; and two mausoleums, the 16th-century Chakh Ali Khan and 17th-century Avgan Muhammed Sultan, where the Tatar princes are buried. Russian art is well represented, too. Around the central square are the churches of St Nicholas (1790–05), Annunciation (1740), Dormition (1753), Trinity (1756–64) and St Elijah (1820–43). Several private mansions (end 18th–early 19th centuries) in late-classic style have been preserved, along with shopping arcades over 200 years old.

Ryazan

Founded on the right bank of the Oka at its confluence with the Trubezh river, this town of 530,000 inhabitants was formerly called Perselav-Ryazanski. Its principal centre of interest is the Museum-Reserve of Architecture and History, one of the oldest in Russia, created on June 15, 1884. Inside the kremlin, originally fortified in 1095 and covering 26 ha of land, is an impressive group of 18 monuments covering nine centuries, from the 11th to the 19th. The most outstanding is the imposing five-domed Dormition Cathedral, the masterpiece of architect Bukhvostov. Even larger than the one in Moscow's Kremlin, it is in Narychkine style. Note the delicate tracery of the cross surmounting the domes, forged by Malofeyev, and the superb white stone sculpture of the façade. Inside, the amazing carved wooden icon screen has four tiers and stands 27 m (88 ft high).

Surmounted by a golden spire, the bell tower (1789–1840) looms over the town. Its four storeys took 50 years to build, by three different architects: Rusko, Thon, Voronikhin. It has, however, retained a unity of style, with rather severe classical lines. Climb up to the viewing platform on the third floor for a magnificent panorama of Ryazan.

Exhibitions are held in five public buildings dating from the 17th century and now restored. Among them is the grand palace of Oleg, 94 m (308 ft) long. There is an original theatre-museum, unique in Russia, where you will learn about the history, culture and nature of the region. Its collections are composed of some 220,000 pieces: silver and gold jewellery of Ryazan ladies of the 12th and 13th centuries, icons from the early 13th century, costumes, ceramics and lace.

The 15th-century Nativity Cathedral, altered several times, can now be considered to be of 19th-century Russian-Byzantine style. It has been returned to the Orthodox Church, and services are held there, though it is still a museum.

Konstantinovo

This village, 43 km (27 miles) from Ryazan on the banks of the Oka, gained fame when Russia's only museum devoted to the life and work of Sergey Essenin was created here in October 1965. A lyrical poet, he was born in Konstantinovo on September 21, 1895, the son of a modest peasant family. He was brought up by his grandparents, and during his childhood learned to appreciate nature and the hardships of country life. These were the subjects that most influenced his poetry, and he referred to himself as "the last country poet". He could not cope with the upheaval caused by the Revolution, and ravaged by alcohol, he slashed his wrists, wrote eight lines of a poem with his blood, then hung himself on December 30, 1925, aged 30. The grounds of the museum contain his parents' isba, which his sisters helped to re-furnish, as well as the primary school where he studied up to 1909. There is also the little church of Our Lady of Kazan (18th century), and the private mansion of Lydia Ivanovna Kachinina, the village's last landowner and the inspiration behind many of Essenin's poems, notably Anna Snegina. He was considered an outcast and his supporters had to fight for his rehabilitation before this museum could be set up.

From Konstantinovo, the boats go directly to Moscow, with no other stops along the way.

The Kama from Kazan to Perm

The Kama has its source in the Urals. It courses for 1,805 km (1,122 miles) and joins the Volga 70 km (43 miles) downriver from Kazan, doubling its flow. It drains 370,000 sq km, with an average flow of 3,900 cu m per second, and remains one of the most important trading routes of eastern Russia.

Nizhnekamsk

In Tatarstan, 237 km (147 miles) from Kazan on the left bank of the Kama, this new town of 222,000 inhabitants was founded in 1966. The first buildings appeared in 1961 with the construction of a vast petrochemical plant. This industrial city produces mainly tyres, and derived chemical and petrochemical products. There are as many Russians as Tatars here, with a 3 per cent Chuvash minority. Russia's biggest mosque was opened in Nizhnekamsk in 1996. Despite all the industry, the town is green and cheerful, surrounded by pine trees and full of parks and gardens.

Elabuga

If you explore the narrow streets of this charming town you will soon come to the museum of the landscape painter Ivan Shishkin (1832–1898), set in his home and furnished with period pieces. You can see his studio, his bedroom and some of his works.

Tchaikovsky

This new industrial town, amid plenty of greenery, was build in 1955 around the Votkinski hydroelectric power plant, on the site of the old village of Saigatka. It was named in 1956 in honour of the composer Piotr Ilyich Tchaikovsky, who was born close by in the little industrial town of Votkinsk. Trips are arranged from here to visit his place of birth, where music festivals are organized.

Votkinsk

In 1935, this large working-class borough was transformed into the important Udmurtia industrial centre; today it has 105,000 inhabitants. In the 18th century iron was mined and smelted on the shores of the Votka. It produced the best anchors in Russia, and the metal beams of the spire of the Peter and Paul Fortress in St Petersburg were forged here. A beautiful museum has been set up in the house where Tchaikovsky was born and spent the first eight years of his childhood. Numerous recitals are held there throughout the year.

Perm

Today a city of 1.1 million inhabitants, Perm was founded in 1723 on the left bank of the Kama by V.N. Tatichev, famous historian and geographer at the time of Peter the Great. On his advice the tsar had a copper smelting works built at the confluence of a small river, the Egoshikha, and the Kama. A town grew up near by, becoming the town of Perm in 1781. By the 19th century it was a typical commercial city at the crossing of the trade routes of Europe and Asia. Today, like all the towns in the Urals, Perm has become an important industrial centre on the Trans-Siberian line, dealing in chemical and petrochemical manufacture, wood and mechanics. Boris Pasternak lived in Perm, and it was here that he wrote Dr Jivago. Among the city sights are the baroque St Peter and St Paul Cathedral (1757–64), the Transfiguration Monastery (1798–1832) with its bell tower (1818–32), and a superb art gallery, housed since 1922 in an old cathedral and today the most important in the region. It contains unique collections of icons of the 16th to 19th centuries, embroidery, woodcarving (17th–19th centuries) and paintings by Russian artists.

Near Perm, the village of Khokhlova has an open-air museum of architecture and folklore.

Cultural Notes

Art Collecting

You may be wondering how so many early works by Matisse and Picasso came to be in the Hermitage and the Pushkin Museum—and who brought all the paintings by Monet, Renoir, Cézanne and Van Gogh to Russia. The credit goes to two rich merchants, Sergey Shchukin and Ivan Morozov.

Shchukin discovered the French Impressionists when he visited Paris in 1897, bought dozens of paintings and displayed them in his Moscow mansion, which he opened to the public on Saturday afternoons. Russia's young painters had scarcely begun to absorb the new influences when Shchukin met Matisse and Picasso. He became the chief patron of Matisse, buying his most important works and bringing the artist to Moscow to install them. Matisse in turn introduced him to Picasso; by 1914 Shchukin had over 50 Picassos in his collection. Morozov concentrated on Cézanne, Monet, Degas, Gauguin and Renoir as well as Matisse.

After the 1917 Revolution, private art collections such as Shchukin's and Morozov's were seized by the state and given to the museums that hold them to this day.

Calendar

How come the October Revolution took place in November 1917? The Julian calendar devised by the Romans gradually fell behind the seasons; in the 18th century the Gregorian version was adopted by most European nations, who skipped 11 days to catch up. But Russia had only just moved to the Julian, and stuck with it until 1918 (by then it was 13 days out) when the new Soviet government made the switch. Historians have to choose between the Old or New Calendars when recording earlier events.

Cameron, Charles

Catherine II knew what sort of building style she liked—the Classical Revival. Failing to find Russian architects to satisfy her, she sent for Charles Cameron on the strength of a book he had written about Roman baths. Cameron claimed to be a Scottish aristocrat, a Jacobite exile from his homeland, but it seems more likely that he was a middle-class Londoner, born in 1740. He studied in Rome in the 1760s; some of his drawings of ancient monuments are preserved at the Engineering Institute in St Petersburg, where he arrived in about 1777. For most of the next 20 years he worked for Catherine, mainly at St Petersburg. He remodelled Rastrelli's Catherine Palace at Tsarskoe Selo, adding the classical sculpture gallery, and built palaces and pavilions at Pavlovsk, the estate presented by Catherine II to her son Paul.

When Paul became tsar, Cameron was dismissed. He returned after Alexander I succeeded his murdered father in 1801 but spent his last ten years on barracks and hospitals, not palaces. He got into financial difficulties and had to sell off his library. His death, probably in 1812, went unnoticed in Britain where nothing to his design was ever built. Most of his drawings survive; they were invaluable aids in the restoration work at Tsarskoe Selo and Pavlovsk after World War II.

Icons

Until the 18th century, Russian painting was a branch of Byzantine art, depicting holy subjects in a stylized form. Arrayed in strict order on the iconostasis separating the congregation from the priests' sanctum, or hanging in separate chapels or shrines, icons were intended to focus the minds of believers. Some were credited with the power to grant prayers or work miracles; famous icons were carried by armies into battle.

The permitted subjects were limited: Christ, the Holy Trinity, the Virgin Mary (generally called the Mother of God in the Russian Church), angels and saints. Favourite saints include Boris and Gleb, martyred sons of Vladimir of Kiev; the monks he invited from Byzantium in the 9th century probably brought the first icons with them. These were copied endlessly by local artists; nothing new was tried until the 12th century, in Novgorod, when faces became less stylized and background colours lighter.

Theophanes the Greek, who arrived from Byzantium in about 1370, brought new drama and expression to the art, but it was his Russian follower Andrey Rublyov who finally broke with the Byzantine formula. Painting in long flowing curves and rich colours— vibrant reds, birchbark whites, sky blues and acid greens—his serene, graceful figures set a new style. Rublyov's *Trinity* (now in the Tretyakov Gallery) became Russia's most popular icon, the model for thousands of copies.

Later artists were tempted to still greater realism, provoking church patriarchs to protest; saints who looked too human might divert the thoughts of the faithful down the wrong path. Originality was suppressed, and to this day icons follow time-honoured formulas.

Pushkin, Alexander

Nothing about the national poet (1799–1837) was ordinary, from his ancestry—his great-grand-father was an Ethiopian prince adopted by Peter the Great—to his early death in a duel, defending his wife's honour. No figure in Russian literature has been more influential, and his works have been the basis of many operas, ballets and films.

Aristocratic families such as Pushkin's spoke French, but his old nurse, a freed serf, taught him the Russian folk tales that influenced his early poems. His radical politics led to exile in Odessa, where he seduced the wife of the governor and fought several duels. On return to Moscow he was hauled before Nicholas I who rightly suspected him of supporting the failed Decembrists' coup, but the tsar was impressed enough to let him off with a warning and the promise—or threat—to act as his personal censor.

Pushkin's famous novel in verse, *Eugene Onegin* (1833), depicts quintessential Russian characters: the disillusioned Onegin, the romantic, doomed Lensky and idealistic Tatyana. *The Bronze Horseman* (1833) evokes St Petersburg and its founder, Peter the Great, who surveys the marshy waste where he intends to found his new city, and foresees the time when "Old Moscow was put in the shade by the younger capital like a purple-clad dowager by a new tsarina."

Russian Impact

Italians built the Kremlin churches in the 15th and 16th centuries; the first court theatre was set up by Germans; French writers so charmed the nobility that they took up the language full time and scarcely spoke their own. Throughout the 18th century under Peter the Great, Anna, Elizabeth and Catherine II, there was a frenzy of borrowing from the West. Then, Russian writers, composers and painters produced a national culture that gained a world audience. Tolstoy's novels and Tchaikovsky's music led the way, but the greatest flowering was in the early 20th century. Kandinsky and Malevich created new art forms, Stravinsky and Prokofiev stunned Paris with their innovative music, Diaghilev's *Ballets Russes* amazed audiences by taking a Western art to new levels of perfection, and Stanislavsky's "method" revolutionized acting technique. Stalin closed the shutters, but after his death a relaxation began. Now with censorship gone, their freedom to travel restored (and needing to earn a living), Russian creative and performing artists are again making a worldwide impact.

Dining Out

To get through the long winters, northern Russia has always relied on preserved foods such as salted or pickled herrings, smoked salmon and gherkins in dill-flavoured vinegar. The brief summer brings fruits and vegetables from the peasants' plots of land and mushrooms from the forests; hunting for them is a local passion. Menus still reflect the old ways, though Italian, Indian, Japanese and international fast food are now gaining ground.

Timing

Hotels serve breakfast (*zavtrak*) from around 7.30 to 9.30 a.m., lunch (*obed* – pronounced *ah-byet*) from noon to 3 p.m. and dinner (*oozhin*) from 6 to 9 p.m. Restaurants and clubs stay open longer.

Breakfast

Local dishes include wheat porridge (*kasha*), pancakes with sour cream (*smetana*), and eggs, hard-boiled or baked in an earthenware pot. Tourist hotels may put on a simple buffet with juice (usually apple or cranberry), cereals, bread and sweet rolls, as well as oddities such as grated carrot and chopped beetroot. Fresh fruit is scarce, except in the top hotels.

Appetizers

The best often comes first in a Russian meal, the form of hot or cold snacks (*zakoosky*). Many are salty, designed to go with drinks. The choice could include pickled mushrooms, smoked salmon, jellied sturgeon or red salmon roe "caviar". Genuine sturgeon's roe caviar (*ikra*) is alarmingly expensive, even in Russia. Connoisseurs reject additives (such as chopped onion), which might interfere with the delicate flavour, and spread the caviar on morsels of lightly toasted white bread spread with unsalted butter. Alternatively, it can be served with *blini* (thin, light pancakes) and sour cream. Vodka is the traditional accompaniment.

Called Russian salad in the West, the mixture of diced carrot and potato, peas, onion, chicken, ham and hard-boiled egg in a creamy dressing is known locally as *salat stalichny* ("capital city salad").

Popular hot starters, also eaten as snacks between meals, include forest mushrooms in a creamy sauce, or sliced chicken in a mini-casserole. *Pirozhki* are bread rolls with a filling, usually of meat.

Soups

Borshch has spread far beyond Russia, but you should be able to find it on its home ground. The Russian type is based on cabbage, but the best-known version, Ukrainian in origin, is made with beetroot (and a lot of other things as well, including meat). It's often served with a delicate cheese pie on the side.

Chicken broth (*boolyon*) can be particularly good when it is served with *pelmeni*, little dumplings made with chopped meat in a thin noodle dough.

Solyanka is a filling meat and vegetable soup, a staple of the menus in *stalovaya* ("dining room") restaurants, an inexpensive option.

Okroshka is a chilled summer soup whose secret ingredient is *kvass*, a slightly alcoholic drink made from fermented rye bread.

Bread

Rye bread, especially the dark sort called black bread (*chyorny khleb*), is the tastiest, but you may have to ask for it in tourist hotels, where it's assumed that foreigners want white.

Main Courses

The fresh fish on offer is usually limited to pike-perch or sturgeon, prepared in various ways and served either plain or with a tangy cream sauce.

A habit copied from the Caucasian republics to the south, *shashlik* is skewered pieces of lamb or mutton and onion, grilled over charcoal and served with a spicy sauce. *Lyulya kebab* is a variation on the same theme—spiced meatballs, skewered and char-grilled.

In the dish known as Beef Stroganov, supposedly invented for Count Stroganov, thin strips of beef tenderloin (or poorer cuts that are often unfortunately substituted) are slowly braised in a tasty sauce of onions and sour cream and served with rice or fried potatoes.

Chicken Kiev, *kotleti pa-kievsky*, is boned chicken breast filled with melted butter. Be careful when you cut into it with your knife as the butter tends to splash out. Another chicken dish (*tsiplyata tabaka*) is made by flattening the bird onto a buttered skillet and cooking it slowly until crisp. Chopped onion and a hot garlic sauce are the usual extras.

Desserts

Ice cream (*morozhenoye*) is the universal—sometimes the only—dessert, possibly garnished with a little fruit. *Oladyi* are pancakes served with jam or cottage cheese and dusted with icing sugar, and *romovaya baba* (like rum baba) is a cake soaked in rum syrup.

Snacks

If you don't want to spend too much time in restaurants, a handy alternative is to follow the example of the Russians and buy something at one of the numerous street stalls, or in the snack shops where you eat standing up (they also sell drinks). You can sample *blinis* (pancakes) or deep-fried *pirozhki*, both with savoury or sweet fillings; *pelmeni* (meat ravioli); *shashlyk* (kebabs); open sandwiches; *chebureki*, Georgian or Armenian deep-fried pastries filled with cheese or mutton; corn on the cob grilled by old ladies at the roadside. There are also biscuits and cream cakes *(torty)*, and chocolates *(konfiety)* wrapped in pretty paper. The best come from Moscow's Krasny Oktiabr factory. Ice cream is sold even on the coldest winter days.

Drinks

Wines from Moldova, Georgia, the Crimea and other parts of the former USSR are not expensive, but the quality is unpredictable. Western European and other imports are available at higher prices in the better hotels, restaurants and on cruise boats. Spark-

---

---

ling wines (*shampanskoye*) from Georgia are mostly sweet—even the one labelled *sukhoye* (dry).

Armenia and Georgia produce brandy (*konyak*) which can be quite good; Russians often drink it as an aperitif.

The local beer (*pivo*) tends to taste yeasty and immature; you may prefer to pay extra for the imported brews. Top hotels and bars have Irish stouts and other famous brands on draught.

Mineral water (*mineralnaya voda*) has an honoured place on Russian tables. *Borzhomi* is the local favourite, but too alkaline for most visitors' tastes.

Coffee (*kofye*) is a disappointment in most places—the long years when substitutes were made from roasted cereals have gone but left their mark in a lack of understanding of what constitutes a good cup of coffee. You may be better off with tea (*chai*). 93

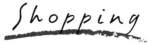

Shopping

A strong craft tradition provides a good choice of souvenirs: painted and lacquered papier-mâché and wood, embroidery and lace. Relics of the Soviet era, such as uniforms and medals are on offer but at rising prices, like a new form of antique. The favourable exchange rate makes CDs and cassettes a bargain.

Where to Shop

Hotel shops give an idea of the range of souvenirs available. You can find the same items in street markets and on stalls near tourist sites, and you should be able to negotiate a substantial discount. GUM, facing Moscow's Red Square, and TsUM, near the Bolshoy Theatre, are full of boutiques selling Russian products as well as luxury imports. Gostiny Dvor on Nevsky Prospekt is St Petersburg's equivalent. Museum shops are a good source of gifts.

Black-clad grannies still spread a few pathetic possessions on the ground, but the privately run kiosks that mushroomed in the early days after the fall of communism are now concentrated in the underground passages leading to Metro stations. Weekend markets, for example in Moscow's Old Arbat area or Ismailovsky Park, are happy hunting grounds, but beware currency scams and pickpockets!

Amber

Amber is the fossilized resin from pine trees, mainly from the Baltic coast. Ranging from pale yellow to gold and deep red, it makes eye-catching bracelets and necklaces, light in weight and warm to the touch. Unless you have an expert on hand, buying it is something of a lottery.

Khokhloma Ware

Spoons, bowls, *kvass* cups, trays and boxes from the village of Khokhloma, bright red and gold designs passed down from father to son, are sold at souvenir shops everywhere. They're made by oiling the wood, painting it with metallic powders, and then varnishing and baking.

Matryoshka Dolls

It's a rare visitor who can resist buying a set of *matryoshka* nesting dolls. Traditional versions — anything from 3 to 35 dolls—are painted as peasant women, each inside the next size up. Now they have been joined by Disney figures, American footballers and Russian Leaders Through the Ages, with an ultimate collection including Ivan the Terrible, Peter the Great, Nicholas II, Lenin, Stalin, Khrushchev and Gorbachev, all contained within a giant Yeltsin—or an outsize Putin.

Miniature Paintings

When the 1917 revolution put icon painters out of business, those in four of the main villages that had specialized in the art turned to painting miniatures on papier-mâché boxes. The design is drawn on paper, which is then pricked with a needle and sprinkled with paint powder to transfer the outline to the box. After painting with the finest brushes, seven layers of varnish are applied. The boxes are sometimes called Palekh ware, after one of the villages. Most designs have a black background.

Paintings

Artists turn out watercolours and drawings of churches and other sights for sale to tourists. Some can be amateurish, but many are beautifully done, and prices are usually very reasonable.

Samovars and Souvenirs

Unusual bygones, candlesticks and samovars turn up on market stalls, though there are few bargains to be found these days. Mementoes of the Soviet Union have become collectors' items. Revolutionary posters are likely to be laser-printed copies. Be wary of icons: if genuine, they may have been stolen, and old ones cannot be exported.

Shawls

Traditional shawls are woven in fine wool with flower patterns. At Volgograd you will see very fine yet warm shawls of goathair, in plain colours.

THE SYSTEM

Many shops still stick to the time-consuming "three queue" method, notorious from the days of Soviet shortages. You line up to see what goods are on sale and find out the price. Then you join another line to reach the cashier's desk (kassa) where you pay and get a receipt. Finally you line up again at the sales counter to hand this over and receive your purchase. This cumbersome arrangement was not a communist creation; it dates from tsarist days. It was devised with the laudable aim of keeping sales assistants' hands unsoiled by germ-laden banknotes and coins.

95

WATERWAYS: VITAL STATISTICS

ST PETERSBURG TO MOSCOW

St Petersburg–Valaam	227 km
Valaam–Petrozavodsk	360 km
Petrozavodsk–Kizhi	70 km
Kizhi–Goritsy	340 km
Goritsy–Yaroslavl	400 km
Yaroslavl–Uglitch	108 km
Uglich–Moscow	266 km

LAKES, CANALS AND RIVERS

Neva	74 km
Lake Ladoga	18,000 sq km
Svir	215 km
Lake Onega	10,000 sq km
Kovya	43 km
White Lake	1,400 sq km
Volga-Baltic Canal	360 km
Sheksna	196 km
Rybinsk Reservoir	4,500 sq km
Volga	3,688 km
Moscow Canal	128 km

FROM MOSCOW TO ASTRAKHAN

Moscow–Uglich	266 km
Uglich–Yaroslavl	131 km
Yaroslavl–Kostroma	76 km
Kostroma–Nizhny Novgorod	308 km
Nizhny Novgorod–Kazan	408 km
Kazan–Simbirsk	228 km
Simbirsk–Samara	213 km
Samara–Saratov	432 km
Saratov–Volgograd	385 km
Volgograd–Nikolskoye	245 km
Nikolskoye–Astrakhan	249 km

The Hard Facts

To help with your travel plans, here are some useful facts about Russia.

Airports

Moscow's main international airport, Sheremetyevo, lies 29 km (18 miles) northwest of the city. Terminal 2 handles international flights, Terminal 1 domestic.

Buses run to the City Air Terminal (some way northeast of the centre) at 30-minute intervals from 5 a.m. to midnight, taking 30–45 minutes. More frequent buses run to the Rechnoy Voksal station on the Metro system. Taxis are much more expensive, but are available at any time; avoid taxi touts and unofficial taxis and be sure to agree the price in advance.

Top hotels and tour operators will arrange in advance for airport transfers for their clients. Companies with desks at the airport can do the same on the spot for independent travellers.

St Petersburg's airport, Pulkovo, lies 17 km (11 miles) south of the city. There are two terminals linked by a shuttle service; check with the airline which one it uses. A bus runs every 10 minutes to the city Aeroflot office near Nevsky Prospekt. Taxis take 30 minutes.

Car Hire

Some of the big international companies are represented in Russia, enquire in your home country before your visit. Local companies also rent cars at airports and in major cities. Whichever you use, check that rates include full insurance against loss and damage, and local taxes. There is usually no limit on the distance you can cover, but an extra charge may be levied for drop-off at a different location, and for additional driver(s).

To rent a car, you need a current driving licence (which you must have held for at least a year) and to be over 21 (25 with some companies). You are expected to pay with a major credit card.

Climate

Summers are hot and sometimes humid, with occasional rain; the day temperature can be more than 30°C (86°F). Winters are famously cold, with frequent snow. Spring brings the thaw of accumulated ice and snow, and can be wet. Autumn is pleasant, but brief, before snowfalls begin again, usually in October.

Clothing

Take lightweight clothing in summer (cotton is most comfortable), with an extra layer for cool evenings. A raincoat, or at least an umbrella, will be useful. In winter, take gloves, a heavy overcoat and waterproof shoes. You can buy a hat on arrival. Go out of doors bare-headed when it's –20°C, and the locals will look at you as if you are mad. Bonnets with wing-like flaps that fold down to form ear-muffs are traditionally for men. For some reason, women's ears are supposed to be immune from freezing.

Shorts and revealing tops are frowned on in the cities (and absolutely banned for church visits). A few more formal restaurants ask men to wear a jacket and tie; some clubs ban jeans.

Communications

The telephone system is beginning to improve, but starting from a notoriously low standard it has a long way to go. To make an international call to Russia, dial the international access code followed by 7 and the area code (including initial 0) and number.

To make an international call from Russia, dial 8, wait for a second dial tone, dial 10 and then the country code (1 for US and Canada, 44 for UK), area code (omitting the initial zero) and number. You can call from public telephone centres at some post offices, paying at the end of the call. Best of all, if you can find one, are the blue card-phones, operated by smart cards available at telephone desks in large hotels.

It generally costs much more to telephone from your hotel room, unless you use one of the calling cards issued by international telephone companies. Fax messages can be sent and received through many hotels.

Cellular phone networks are spreading fast. Check with the service provider in your home country to see if your mobile phone will work in Russia.

Postal services work, although slowly. Airmail reaches most European destinations in five to seven days. As well as main post offices, there are small branches in tourist hotels, and shops that sell postcards may also have stamps. Moscow's main post office is at 7 Tverskaya Street; St Petersburg's is near St Isaac's Cathedral, Pochtamtskaya Street.

Consulates and Embassies

American Embassy
   Bolshoy Devyatinskiy,
   Pereulok 8, Moscow
   tel. (095) 728 5000

American Consulate
   Furshtadtskaya ul. 15
   St Petersburg
   tel. (0812) 331 2600

British Embassy
Smolenskaya nab. 10, Moscow
tel. (095) 956 7200

British Consulate
Pl. Proletarskoy Diktatury 5
St Petersburg
tel. (0812) 320 3200

Canadian Embassy
Starokonyushenny per. 23
Moscow
tel. (095) 105 6000

Irish Embassy
Grokholsky per. 5, Moscow
tel (095) 937 5911

Driving

Even some major roads are poorly surfaced; minor roads may be appalling. Driving in cities can be frustrating, with difficult one-way systems, few parking places, and policemen ready to swoop down on foreigners with a fine for no apparent reason. Drinking and driving is strictly prohibited.

Drive on the right and always park pointing in the same direction as the traffic. Seat belts must be worn. Speed limits for cars are 50 kph (31 mph) in built-up areas, 90–100 kph (56–62 mph) outside towns, 120 kph (75 mph) on major highways unless otherwise marked. GAI police patrol in cars and stand at major junctions. If you have an accident, try to inform the police, or ensure that someone else does. If anyone is injured, you may be arrested until blame is allocated. If you take your own vehicle, make certain that you are fully insured. (Check with your insurance company or motoring organization.) A national licence with an authorized translation, or an international driving licence, is required.

Emergencies
To call the Police dial 02; the Fire Service 01, for an Ambulance 03.

Etiquette
Don't be put off by apparent rudeness. An ingrained suspicion of strangers persists, as does the negative attitude of many minor officials, ticket clerks and doormen. You may succeed in warming them with a smile and a greeting—or you may not. Young people are much more open and friendly. It's usual to shake hands when introduced.

Formalities
Visas (which are expensive) are required by all visitors. Tour companies apply for visas on behalf of their clients; up to five weeks may be needed. Independent travellers should obtain application forms from Russian embassies and follow the instructions given. In all cases, three passport photographs must be supplied. Cruise ship passengers

may be allowed to land without obtaining visas in advance, but it can save time if you have one.

After a stay of three days, your passport and visa have to be officially registered. Large hotels will do this for you. Carry photocopies of your passport, visa and ticket to ease problems in case of loss.

Foreign currency up to the equivalent of US$10,000 can be imported but must be declared on arrival, as well as any valuable items such as cameras, laptop computers and jewellery. These will be listed on a customs declaration form. Make sure it is officially stamped, and keep it safe to show on departure.

Travellers over 16 may import the following amounts duty-free:
– 1000 cigarettes or
– 1 kg tobaccco products;
– 1.5 litres alcoholic beverages
– 2 litres wine;
– a reasonable quantity of perfume for personal use.
You can buy duty-free goods on arrival at Russia's main international airports.

Health

Be sure to take sunscreen cream with a high protection factor (at least 20), dark glasses and any medicines you may need: the same brands may not be available. Insect repellent will be useful in summer, especially if you'll be in the countryside, on the rivers or in the north where mosquitoes can be a menace.

Typhoid, tetanus and polio vaccinations should be up to date, though they are not compulsory. AIDS tests are required for long-stay visitors (over three months).

You should have comprehensive travel insurance, including provision for medical expenses. Proof of cover is usually required before a visa is issued. UK and most EU residents can obtain free emergency treatment in Russia by showing their passports.

Language

Russian is the national language. English is quite widely understood, but if you try to learn and use a few phrases in Russian, your efforts will be appreciated.

А	a	П	p
Б	b	Р	r
В	v	С	s
Г	g	Т	t
Д	d	У	u
Е	e	Ф	f
Ж	zh	Х	kh
З	z	Ц	ts
И	i	Ч	tch
Й	y	Ш	ch
К	k	Щ	shch
Л	l	Ы	y
М	m	Э	e
Н	n	Ю	yu
О	o	Я	ya

Media

State-run and commercial TV channels are augmented in the top international hotels by satellite and cable channels, including BBC World, NBC and Eurosport.

Newspapers in English, the daily *Moscow Times*, the *Moscow Tribune*, the *St Petersburg Times* and *St Petersburg Press* (weekly) are widely available. The UK and other western European papers arrive by early evening on the day of publication.

Money

The currency is the *rouble* (RUB or p.), divided into 100 *kopeks* (k.), with coins ranging from 1k. to 5 roubles and banknotes from 5 to 500 roubles.

Foreign currency and travellers cheques (US dollar cheques are best) may be changed at banks or the exchange desk to be found in the larger hotels. It is illegal to change other than at an official exchange, apart from the risk of being given counterfeit or out-of-date roubles. Keep the receipts to show on departure, and do not change large amounts at any one time. The currency was reformed in 1997, one new rouble taking the place of 1,000 old ones; both sets of banknotes stayed in use, but various valueless notes are still around.

US dollar bills are widely accepted by traders, at the current rate of exchange, although this is technically illegal. Major credit cards are accepted only at major hotels, some restaurants and a few Western-style shops. Using them or bank cards, cash may be obtained from ATMs (automatic teller machines) outside big city banks, if you know your PIN, but be vigilant.

Opening Hours

Banks open Monday to Friday 9.30 a.m.–5.30 p.m. Airport and other exchange offices keep longer hours.

Post offices open Monday to Friday 8.30 a.m.–2.30 p.m., Saturdays 9.30 a.m.–1 p.m.

Most shops open Monday to Saturday 9 a.m.–5 p.m. Some open at 8 a.m. and big city stores may stay open Tuesday to Friday until 9 p.m.

Museums and other attractions generally open at 9.30 or 10 a.m. and close around 5.30 p.m. (later in summer). Some close on Mondays, and many close 1.30–4 p.m. It's worth trying to find out in advance.

Photography and Video

Colour film and some brands of transparency film are available in the cities. Colour prints can be processed locally but quality cannot be guaranteed. Transparency film is best taken back to your own country for processing.

Videotape is available. Pre-recorded tapes are compatible with most of Europe, but not the US.

Public Holidays

January 1–2	New Year
January 7	Russian Orthodox Christmas
February 23	Defenders of the Motherland
March 8	International Women's Day
March or April	Orthodox Easter
May 1–2	May Day
May 9	Victory Day
June 12	Independence Day
August 22	National Flag Day
November 7	Anniversary of the October Revolution
December 31	New Year's Eve

If a holiday falls on a Saturday or Sunday, the following Monday is taken off instead.

Public Transport

The most efficient way of getting around Moscow and St Petersburg is by Metro. The Moscow stations are clean, resplendent works of art in marble and gilt, and those of St Petersburg only slightly less magnificent. They are marked outside by a big M sign. Buy a card from the window inside the entrance, insert it in the automatic gate, which will open to let you through. If you need to change lines, follow the passages indicated by blue signs (Pere-khod) showing a figure going up the stairs. Exits are marked Vykhod v Gorod. The name of the next station is announced as the doors close.

Bus stops are marked A, tram and trolley T. Tickets are sold in kiosks at major stations.

Taxis are usually available. Even if they have meters, the drivers will often claim that they don't work, or that the fare they show must be multiplied by some large factor, so agree the fare in advance.

Bus companies run regular services between all the main cities and towns, starting from central bus stations or railway stations.

Trains are a cheaper and more interesting way of travelling between cities than flying. Sleeping cars are provided on longer journeys (two-berth in 1st class, four-berth in 2nd class), including the 11-hour overnight Moscow–St Petersburg route.

Religion

Most Russians are atheists, the way they were brought up, but attendance at Orthodox churches is increasing among the younger generation. Many churches have been re-opened, and priests, monks and nuns are often seen in public—something unheard of in the USSR. Other sects are active in trying to gain converts.

For the large foreign population, resident and transient, there are various churches, synagogues and mosques in Moscow and St Petersburg. Times of services are listed in the local English-language press.

Security
Street crime in the cities is a problem, so take normal precautions: avoid dark or lonely places at night, beware of pickpockets in crowded places; don't carry large amounts of cash or wear valuable jewellery. Don't leave anything on show when parking a car. Use guarded parks if you can, remove the car radio and leave the glove box open—and empty. Leave *nothing* in a car overnight.

Time
Western Russia is on GMT +3, advancing to GMT +4 between April and October.

Tipping
Waiters in privately run restaurants, bars and clubs have come to expect a tip of about 10 per cent. Taxi fares are generally agreed in advance and no tip is added; meter fares can be rounded up by about 10 per cent. A small tip is usually given to porters and cloakroom attendants unless there's a standard charge.

Toilets
Apart from a few where you have to pay, public lavatories are usually in a repellent state, and almost never have paper. Even those at restaurants may be distinctly unpleasant. Good hotels are the best bet. Unless the usual symbols are used, men's rooms are marked with an M, women's with the Russian ZH.

Tourist Information
The formerly state-run Intourist organization has split into many private and local companies. Major tourist hotels may have leaflets about local attractions and city maps, which you can also find in the free magazine *Where – Moscow* and English-language newspapers such as *Neva News* (St Petersburg).

Voltage
The electrical supply is 220V, 50 Hz, AC. Plugs are of the European type, with two round pins. Any 110V equipment needs a transformer as well as an adaptor.

Water
Tap water is safe to drink in Moscow and major international hotels but often tastes chlorinated and metallic, so many people prefer bottled mineral water. Elsewhere, stick to filtered, purified or bottled water—check that the seal is unbroken.

INDEX

GENERAL EDITOR
Barbara Ender-Jones
TEXT
Martin Gostelow
Claude Hervé-Bazin
Anne Kanjounzeff
LAYOUT
Luc Malherbe
PHOTOS CREDITS
Othmar Attiger: p. 1;
Hémisphères/Wysocki:
front cover, pp. 6, 44, 50, 52, 58;
Hémisphères/Verdeil: pp. 4, 16;
Rachel Cavassini: pp. 13, 20–21;
Bildagentur Huber/Gräfenhain:
back cover, pp. 14, 32, 37, 38,
41, 60, 62, 68–69;
Maud Mabillard: p. 2;
Mark Wadlow: p. 18;
David Toaser: p. 24;
Siegfried Layda: p. 27;
jjkphoto.ch: p. 47
Anne Kanjounzeff: pp. 74, 76,
80, 83
MAPS
JPM Publications;
Huber Kartographie

Printed In Switzerland
Weber/Bienne (CTP) — 04/03/01
Edition 2004–2005

Kostroma
Kozelino
Kr.
Profintern
Sergeytsevo
Nekrasovskoye
Nerekhta
Kosmynino
Burmakino
Dulyapino
Podozerskiy
Pistsovo
Oktyabr'skiy
Komsomol'sk
Markovo
Teykovo
Nerl'
Nov.
Leushino
Suzdal'
Nerl'
Tutayev
Norskoye
Tvercy
Krasny
Tkachi
Kotorosl'
Gavrilov
Yam
Oktyabr'skiy
Il'inskoye-
Khovanskoye
Petrovskiy
Gavrilov
Posad
Yur'yev-
Pol'skiy
Yaroslavl
Velikoye
Boriso-
glebskiy
Semibratovo
Oz. Nero
Poreche-
Rybnoye
Sima
Ivankovskiy
Konstantinovskiy
Varegovo
Rostov
Veliky
Ryazan-
cevo
Berendeevo
Balakirevo
Bol.
Selo
Ilinskoye
Petrovskoye
Petrovskoye
Pereslavl-
Zalessky
Volga
Nov.
Nekouz
Myshkino
Uglich
Volga
Oz.
Pleshchevo Zalesskoye
Nagor'e
Kubrinsk
Bogorodskoye
Kalyazin
Nerl'
Oktyabr'
Sonkovo
Kesova
Gora
Kashin
Bely
Gorodok
Severny
Verbilki
Goricy
Kimry
Taldom
Dubna
Tempy
Zaprudnya
Moscow C
Konakovo
Dmitrova
Gora

N

**AROUND
MOSCOW**

0   40 km

0   25 miles

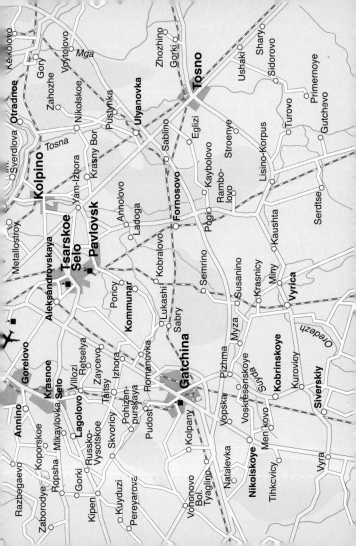

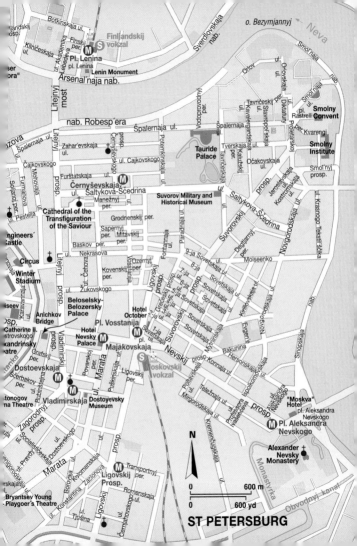

St Petersburg Metro
Санкт Петербургское метро

КОМЕНДАНТСКИЙ ПРОСПЕКТ
Komendantsky Prospekt

ПАРНАССКАЯ
Parnasskaya

ДЕВЯТКИНО
Devyatkino

ГРАЖДАНСКИЙ ПРОСПЕ
Grazhdansky Prospekt

СТАРАЯ ДЕРЕВНЯ
Staraya Derevnya

ПРОСПЕКТ ПРОСВЕЩЕНЬЯ
Prospekt Prosveshchenya

АКАДЕМИЧЕСКАЯ
Akademicheskaya

КРЕСТОВСКИЙ ОСТРОВ
Krestovsky Ostrov

ОЗЕРКИ
Ozerki

ПОЛИТЕХНИЧЕСКАЯ
Politekhnicheskaya

ЧКАЛОВСКАЯ
Chkalovskaya

УДЕЛЬНАЯ
Udelnaya

ПЛ.МУЖЕСТВА
Pl. Muzhestva

ТУЧКОВ МОСТ
Tuchkov Most

ПИОНЕРСКАЯ
Pionerskaya

ЛЕСНАЯ
Lesnaya

ПРИМОРСКАЯ
Primorskaya

ЧЁРНАЯ РЕЧКА
Chernaya Rechka

ВЫБОРГСКАЯ
Vyborgskaya

ПЕТРОГРАДСКАЯ
Petrogradskaya

ПЛ.ЛЕНИНА
Pl. Lenina

ВАСИЛЕОСТРОВСКАЯ
Vasileostrovskaya

ГОРЬКОВСКАЯ
Gorkovskaya

Finland Station

Neva

ЧЕРНЫШЕВСКАЯ
Chernyshevskaya

НЕВСКИЙ ПРОСПЕКТ
Nevsky Prospekt

МАЯКОВСКАЯ
Mayakovskaya

АДМИРАЛТЕЙСКАЯ
Admiralteyskaya

ГОСТИНЫЙ ДВОР
Gostiny Dvor

ПЛ.ВОССТАНИЯ
Pl. Vosstania

ВЛАДИМИРСКАЯ
Vladimirskaya

Moscow Station

САДОВАЯ
Sadovaya

ДОСТОЕВСКАЯ
Dostojevskaya

СЕННАЯ ПЛ.
Sennaya Pl.

ПУШКИНСКАЯ
Pushkinskaya

ЛИГОВСКАЯ
Ligovskaya

ПЛ. АЛЕКСАНДРА НЕВСКОГ
Pl. Alexandra Nevskogo

ТЕХНОЛОГИЧЕСКИЙ ИНСТИТУТ
Tekhnologichesky Institut

Vitebsk Station

ФРУНЗЕНСКАЯ
Frunzenskaya

Obvodnyy

Warsaw Station
Baltic Station

БАЛТИЙСКАЯ
Baltyskaya

ЕЛИЗАРОВСКАЯ
Elizarovskaya

НОВОЧЕРКАССКАЯ
Novocherkasskaya

НАРВСКАЯ
Narvskaya

МОСКОВСКИЕ ВОРОТА
Moskovskie Vorota

ЛОМОНОСОВСКАЯ
Lomonosovskaya

ЛАДОЖСКАЯ
Ladozhskaya

КИРОВСКИЙ ЗАВОД
Kirovsky Zavod

ЭЛЕКТРОСИЛА
Elektrosila

ПРОСПЕКТ БОЛЬШЕВИКОВ
Prospekt Bolshevikov

АВТОВО
Avtovo

ПАРК ПОБЕДЫ
Park Pobedy

ПРОЛЕТАРСКАЯ
Proletarskaya

УЛ. ДЫБЕНКО
Ulitsa Dybenko

ЛЕНИНСКИЙ ПРОСПЕКТ
Leninsky Prospekt

МОСКОВСКАЯ
Moskovskaya

ЗВЁЗДНАЯ
Zvezdnaya

ОБУХОВО
Obukhovo

ПРОСПЕКТ ВЕТЕРАНОВ
Prospekt Veteranov

КУПЧИНО
Kupchino

РЫБАЦКОЕ
Rybaskoye

● *Transfer Station*

■ *Railway Station*

Line 1 ▬▬▬ *Kirovsko-Vyborgskaya Line* **Line 3** ▬▬▬ *Nevsko-Vasileostrovskaya Line*

Line 2 ▬▬▬ *Moskovsko-Petrogradskaya Line* **Line 4** ▬▬▬ *Pravoberezhnaya Line*

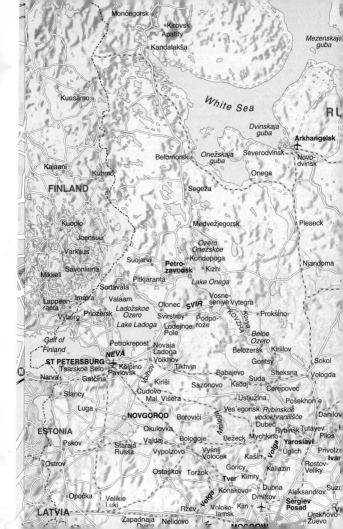